Soldier On

SAM KNOWLES, B SQUADRON 16TH/5TH LANCERS

Soldier On

The Personal Experiences of a Tank
Crewman in the 16th/5th Lancers During
the Second World War

S W Knowles

LEONAUR

Soldier On
The Personal Experiences of a Tank Crewman in the 16th/5th Lancers During the
Second World War
by S W Knowles

FIRST EDITION

Leonaur is an imprint
of Oakpast Ltd

ISBN: 978-1-78282-604-0 (hardcover)
ISBN: 978-1-78282-605-7 (softcover)

http://www.leonaur.com

Publisher's Notes

The views expressed in this book are not necessarily
those of the publisher.

Contents

"Dear Mother
It's a bugger
Sell the pig
And buy me out"
★★★★★★

"Dear Son
It's a bugger
The pig's dead
Soldier on!"

British Army Other Ranks catch phrase
dating from 1910

Foreword

by Colonel Henry Brooke MC
Troop Leader, B Squadron 16th/5th Lancers, Italy 1943-1945
Colonel, 16th/5th The Queen's Royal Lancers, 1980-1985

It gives me great pleasure to write this foreword to Sam Knowles's excellent account of the time we spent together in 'B' Squadron of the 16th/5th Lancers in the Italian campaign from 1943 to 1945. It is not often that tank warfare is described by one of its crewmen, and certainly not in such a readable way.

As readers of Sam's book will quickly realise this campaign was a hard slog from start to finish, with few large scale operations. Rather it was daily small scale operations, normally in support of our infantry, against a stubborn and well led opposition who, it has to be said, made the most of the difficult, mountainous terrain to carry out an extremely effective series of delaying positions the length of Italy.

The lot of the tank crewman in Italy was one of not knowing when you would be hit by any number of weapons from artillery and anti-tank guns to enemy tanks and mines. There was certainty that it would happen, but not when, although those days of being the lead tank were always to be feared most. Sam has described this monotonous grind extremely well, from the death and destruction to the daily routine of keeping the show on the road, both men and machines. On top of all this he brings out the humour of the British soldier when under severe pressure, and which has stood him in such good stead over considerable time.

The Roll of Honour illustrates the price that was paid by the 16th/5th Lancers in the Italian campaign, a similar price of course that was borne by every other Allied fighting unit. Sam's book is another fine tribute to all those in the Regiment who fought with such endless courage and determination, but also to those who did not come home from Italy, ensuring that their sacrifice will not be forgotten.

H. A. G. Brooke, 2016

Northern Italy, 2nd of May, 1945

I was drifting off to sleep when I first heard it—the drone of an approaching aircraft. There came a moment's anxiety, then I remembered the momentous news of that day and once again relaxed. The Second World War as it was fought in Italy had come to an end and that probably meant I need not fear the sound of any aircraft ever again. I was lying wrapped in my blankets, in the shadow of the tank, in an orchard a couple of hundred yards from the banks of the River Po and I couldn't believe my luck. I had actually survived the war!

Unbidden thoughts came flooding in to my mind. Now that sleep was out of the question I sat up and lit a cigarette. As the sound of the passing aircraft faded away, taking with it the harsher realities of my life during wartime, I reflected upon my experiences of the previous few years and tried to imagine the future.

I was just 22 years of age, skilled in radio telegraphy, the use of weapons of destruction and living efficiently in holes in the ground.

How did it all begin?

CHAPTER 1

Going for a Soldier

The Second World War between Great Britain and Germany was declared on 3rd of September, 1939. I was a 16 year old English schoolboy at the time, living with my parents in Hyde, Cheshire. In fact, a little over a week had elapsed since I had received notification that I had obtained my School Certificate. This essential landmark of academic success punctuated the end of my initial secondary school education and opened any number of doors of possibilities for my future. That was about to change.

I was visiting my grandparents at their home in Hyde on that momentous early autumn Sunday morning. As we listened to Prime Minister Neville Chamberlain's radio broadcast informing us that the nation was once again at war with Germany we all naturally felt apprehensive about what would be soon likely to follow. I think we all sensed these events heralded a time of great change and that the world as we knew it would never be the same again.

Of course, everyone expected the country to be continually bombed by the Luftwaffe without delay. Had we not learned of the terrible fate of the Basque city of Guernica, bombed by aircraft of Hitler's Condor Legion and Mussolini's Legionary Air Force during the Spanish Civil War? The pundits of the press had warned us that the loss of life and destruction of cities and towns that the Spanish people had suffered, dreadful though it was, would pale into insignificance compared to what we might expect to befall us in a larger European conflict.

As it transpired what actually immediately happened was very little—so began the so called 'Phoney War' which lasted for a period of some months during which time virtually nothing warlike occurred so far as most of the home population was concerned. This interlude of apparent limbo seemed to surprise everyone we knew and produced an atmosphere of unreality in everyday living which was heightened by a tendency for false optimism. For many people it probably seemed that the future would not actually turn out to be so bleak as many of us had initially feared it would be.

So life went on fairly much as usual.

I returned to The Hyde County Grammar School to study for my Higher School Certificate on the day appointed for the arrival of students, but instead of rejoining the routine of school life which had become so familiar, I discovered that everything about the place appeared to be in a state of disruption. There was, of course, a great deal of uncertainty about what the future might hold as it regarded the operation of the school and much reorganisation to be done to put the place, in its own way, upon a wartime footing. Windows and doors had to be 'blacked-out' as a precaution against the revealing of electric lights which might guide enemy aircraft seeking ground targets. Air Raid Patrols and their facilities were being organised and so on. Most of the classes of younger children were temporarily sent home whilst all this was going on, but we 'sixth-formers', who were the most mature of the school's students, were found useful work to do that might assist the process.

The headmaster approached me and asked me if I would reorganise the school library so I spent a couple of weeks sorting, reclassifying and coding books.

Eventually everything at the school was organised to satisfaction, a new syllabus was issued, and given the circumstances, the school resumed its activities with a semblance of normality. Perhaps that state of affairs might have been practicable for many students, but I knew school life would not long work for me. I felt certain that now that a war was in progress my further education at this point would be a waste of time and, in any event, was destined to be curtailed since I was sure to be called up for military service before much time had elapsed.

I explained my position to the headmaster of my school and asked him if he could use his influence to find me a paying job. There was no careers advice service in those days, however the school headmaster by virtue of his position at the heart of the community, had contacts with local employers and invariably tried to match suitable candidates to appropriate vacancies as they arose.

He went to work on my account and in consequence I was offered of a position with a chartered accountancy practice in Manchester, but that job held no appeal for me at the time, so I turned it down. I was then offered a job with ICI (Rexine) Limited in Newton which I accepted and I began work in the post-room of that company on the 8th of March 1940. The next two years constituted, from my perspective, a period of marking time until my inevitable military conscription 'call-up' which would arrive when I became 18 years old. Nevertheless, I was awarded a couple of minor promotions whilst working at ICI, eventually becoming a cashier's clerk.

★★★★★★

The war, of course, did eventually reach us at home in the form of German bomber aircraft in our skies. The Luftwaffe actually raided Scotland in an attempt to damage the Royal Navy fleet at Rosyth very soon after war was declared in 1939, but Manchester had its first experience of '*blitzkrieg*' on the 8th of August in 1940. The north-west of the country, which of course included the nearby city of Liverpool, received intensive attention from bomber attacks from that time onwards since both cities were vitally important ports and centres of industry. The month of December, brought an escalation to the bombing and the period that became known as 'The Manchester Blitz'. The heaviest raids occurred in the nights from the 22nd of December onwards.

Several bombs fell on my home town of Hyde, causing a number of fatalities and a considerable amount of damage to buildings and property. The last raid of this intensive deluge ended at around midnight on the 23rd/24th of December, which we, perhaps optimistically given the nature of our enemy, thought at the time indicated a Christmas season truce.

In any event, the city had undergone a serious baptism of fire. Nearly 700 people had been killed and over 2,000 had been wounded in the course of these attacks. Over the period of these few days up to 270 enemy aircraft had dropped nearly 500 tons of high explosives and 2000 incendiary bombs upon us. Nazi propaganda claimed that the city had 'been burnt to the ground'. That it had been badly damaged was beyond dispute, but in fact, both the city and the Mancunians were still there and open for business. Propaganda, by its very nature, tends to exaggerate success at the expense of inconvenient facts.

★★★★★★

I was involved in fire watching at this time as my part of the war effort. For those of us at ICI who had fire-watching duties duty rotas were posted in the office. Our responsibilities required that we remained on the business premises from the end of the working day, throughout the night until about 6 am on the following morning. This was practically a daily dusk-to-dawn routine since the German bomber aircraft only operated during the hours of darkness. Through some nights we managed to sleep without any disturbance, but if an air raid warning was sounded we had to patrol the industrial buildings and the site to discover if any incendiary bombs had been dropped within the boundary.

During my time as fire-watcher no bombs fell on our factory which was really just as well for those of us charged with maintaining a presence within it whilst they did so, since there was a considerable quantity of explosive and combustible material stored in and around the place.

Although the normal peace time manufacturing output of the factory was leather-cloth for upholstery used by motorcar manufacturers, the furniture trade and bookbinders, one of the wartime production variations was the manufacture of fabric for barrage balloons. I can still vividly recall the overpowering smell of acetone in the fabric that was produced in our factory and I understood very well the reaction caused by that chemical's exposure to naked flame.

★★★★★★

By this time, I was becoming impatient for my eighteenth birthday to arrive so that I would join the armed services.

One of my best friends was Cecil Procter, the son of a local vicar, Arthur Procter who was, incidentally, a First World War recipient of the Victoria Cross which he won in 1916 in France at Ficheux during the 'Big Push' of the Battle of the Somme whilst serving with the King's (Liverpool) Regiment.

Cecil was a year older than I was and so had already departed to join the RAF and had quickly earned his 'wings'. Cecil returned to his home on leave in March 1941 and we were able to meet for a brief reunion. After our goodbyes were said on that occasion I never saw him again—in July 1941 he was posted missing on flying operations and it was later confirmed that he had been killed in action.

Not uncommonly in those days, but notable for those for whom it might be beyond imagining, both father and son had gone into battle against Germany. The father had, despite his own trials, then had to suffer the loss of his child killed whilst fighting this same foe. Most tragically, on neither occasion did the nation to which they belonged provoke hostilities. Notwithstanding that this was a closely felt and sobering reminder that war could be a dangerous and often fatal affair it little dampened my enthusiasm for joining the army.

Having reached the prescribed age, I duly registered, underwent my medical examination and was instructed to report to the General Service Corps at the 32nd Infantry Training Centre located in Beverley, East Yorkshire on Thursday the 2nd of July 1942.

I was about to embark on my career as a soldier of the British Army.

CHAPTER 2

Take One Young Man

The General Service Corps was the British Army's attempt to rid itself of the justified reputation that it was such a poor adjudicator of its own human resources that it would thrust the proverbial 'square peg into the round hole' heedless of how impractical or unsuitable the outcome might ultimately reveal itself to be. With the introduction of the GSC, instead of posting new recruits haphazardly to regiments and corps that might have vacancies for them regardless of any other consideration, it was decided that all new recruits should spend six weeks in basic training, during which time they would be tested, observed, assessed and finally, hopefully, found the most suitable position for their temperaments and abilities. Perhaps inevitably the army approached this ostensibly sensible initiative in the same infamous fashion that it had diligently managed the flawed system it was intended to replace. The outcome was, therefore, predictable.

★★★★★★

Today almost everyone understands the concept of culture shock. The phrase may be a comparatively new one, but there is nothing new about the experience. In 1942 I was a teenager transported from the familiarity, comforts and liberties of home and civilian life into the unique and hellish world of basic training in the British Army. Despite all the experiences in wartime which were later to come my way I think I can confidently claim that those six weeks constituted the most miserable days of my entire life.

We recruits were hounded in time honoured fashion from the call of reveille in the early morning to 'lights-out' at night as we collapsed into our beds. The time in between these two notable points in every day was filled with what seemed to be an endless round of assault courses and interminably long physical training sessions. We endured hours of this torture including the requirement to hurl ourselves through (yes, through!) hawthorn hedges, circle the noxious interiors of choking gas chambers without the protection of gas-masks; thereafter whilst still gasping from lack of clean air we were forced to run for a mile bearing the weight standard British Army infantry equipment about our bodies.

These were just some of the delights recruits were served courtesy of those who ruled our new existence which made me long for the previously unappreciated boring comforts of my previous life. Meal times brought little respite or consolation, for I genuinely believe that if the food we were given had been doled out to prisoners of war, their rights under the terms of the Geneva Convention would have been justifiably invoked. Nevertheless, despite the fact we were battered, bruised and gastronomically abused we eventually became incredibly physically fit which was, of course, the objective of it all.

I can only imagine that I acquitted myself close to expectations since I was surprised to hear from my platoon sergeant that my name had been put forward as someone who was potentially officer material.

Eventually this six weeks of not-so-refined torture came to an inevitable and welcome conclusion and in the latter part of the final week we were all called to Company Office where we were interviewed individually concerning our military futures.

As I stood before my own interrogator, a major from the training course staff, I recalled some telling advice I had been given a few weeks previously from someone who I had every reason to believe knew what he was talking about. The son of our home's next door neighbours had, in the early 1930s, enlisted in the Lancashire Fusiliers and spent several years serving in India. He had progressed upwards through the ranks, had been eventually commissioned, and was by 1942 a captain and second-in-command of a squadron of the 111th Regiment, Royal Armoured Corps stationed somewhere in Nottinghamshire. As he was on leave at the time I received my orders to report to Beverley, I asked his advice on which branch of the army I should opt for, assuming I was given any choice in the matter.

His reply was uncompromising and left little room for confusion on my part.

"The Ordnance Corps or Signals," he advised emphatically, "but whatever you do, keep away from the bloody tanks!"

Message received and understood NO TANKS! The major glanced through my file, nodding approvingly. This was an encouraging beginning.

"Well, your report is very satisfactory, and now we have to decide your future," he continued, "Have you any preference as to where you would like to go from here?"

"I was thinking of either the Ordnance Corps or the Royal Signals, sir," I replied confidently.

The effect this statement had upon him would scarcely have been more profound if I had suggested my joining the all-female ranks of the Army Territorial Service.

"Nonsense, laddie," he exclaimed, "A fine, strong, fit chap like you doesn't want to be spending the war sitting on his backside behind the lines! We need you up at the front—giving Hitler a bloody nose, eh? No, I shall send you to the 51st Training Regiment, Royal Armoured Corps at Catterick. I'm sure you'll do very well. Goodbye and good luck!"

So, that was that. I stumbled out of his office in a daze though in possession of exactly the kind of military career I had been specifically warned, at all perils, to avoid!

Outside I met my friend, Alan Edmondson—a six feet four-inch rugby football forward who was actually built like a tank. We, of course, compared notes.

"What did you get, Alan?" I asked.

20

"Radio Telephone Operator's Office, Clitheroe Station," he replied, smirking as well he might. As it happened Alan lived about half a mile from Clitheroe railway station and so could confidently contemplate spending his war planning troop train movements and stamping overdue leave passes for soldiers delayed by shortages in the quantities of trains required to convey them. Fortune had ironically delivered this natural warrior to the most comfortable of domestic duties imaginable.

I, by contrast, was bound for armoured warfare despite my preferences for more gentle pursuits. So much for the GSC and the army's new policy of ensuring that square pegs never found themselves shoe-horned into round holes.

On the following Thursday morning, in company with about half a dozen apprehensive 'pegs' bound for 'holes' into which they might not easily fit, I was despatched on the next stage of my military journey.

CHAPTER 3

The Cladding in Armour

Catterick Camp in Yorkshire was an enormous British Army military establishment. Apparently, it was always intended to house a huge concentration of troops and their equipment when the site was originally selected in 1908 by Robert Baden Powell, who became famous for founding the international scouting movement. It was possible to drive through it for miles without seeing a civilian. Unit signs proliferated directing the visitor down neat tarmac roads lined with single-storey brick barrack blocks. It seemed as though every unit in the British Army had a presence there.

Our small cadre was bound for the 51st Training Regiment's base situated at Aisne Lines.

★★★★★★

Most locations within the camp traditionally bore the names of notable engagements from the history of British warfare. This one, tellingly, was of First World War vintage: a desperate battle fought in France only 28 years previously during the early months of the conflict to throw back the armies of the same enemy nation we were now once again fighting as they swept towards Paris.

★★★★★★

On my arrival I was allocated to 138Y Squad which was composed of men gathered together from different GSC units located all over the country. Our instructor was called Sergeant Taylor, a taciturn martinet of an NCO, who in spite of his severity as it was applied, our military training was fair to all and earned our respect if not the warmth of our affections over the following months.

We were given a stern induction speech by a warrant officer who warned us that we would find the training harder than we could imagine, but would be expected to adapt to its demands and to subsequently pass out at the end of the course with honours. This was not a particularly promising start particularly since Catterick Camp together with the other principal army camp at Aldershot did not have the reputations for fostering fond remembrances among their former inhabitants.

However, notwithstanding these ominous auguries, I admit that I thoroughly enjoyed my time at Catterick. After my gruelling training experiences at Beverley, the tough training schedule which had been promised for us at Catterick was by contrast something of a pushover. The syllabus was varied—all tank men would be required of necessity to be able to undertake each crew member's role in the event of an emergency, so we were taught to drive, operate a wireless set including Morse Code, fire the tank's guns on the ranges and to read maps.

In addition, we were introduced to a more inventive type of physical training exercise than most of us had hitherto experienced. The colonel of the regiment was very keen on route marches and almost every Saturday morning saw us on parade at 04:00hrs, prior to foot-slogging 20 miles or so across the North Yorkshire moors. At about 08:00hrs we would typically rendezvous with the cookhouse truck which was there to deliver us an *alfresco* breakfast. Various amusing (for someone) diversions for us were arranged to entertain us *en route*. On one notable occasion we were required to ford a river within 50 yards of a perfectly serviceable bridge. The water came over our waists as we waded across this river and since this excursion took place in late November it was naturally practically freezing cold. Our complaints at this ill treatment were rewarded by a forced march of two miles to dry us out.

★★★★★★

Forty years later, as we watched the news coverage of 'The Falklands War' on our television screens we saw the long lines of the Parachute Regiment and others wending their way towards Port Stanley. That tough progression was then referred to as 'yomping' and was presented almost as something of the modern soldier's own invention. Irrespective of the name given to it I can attest from personal experience that this kind of hard marching under heavy burdens was far from a new phenomenon for the British soldier or, indeed, for any foot soldier of any age in all probability.

★★★★★★

Incidentally, on this particular weekend I undertook what I still think was a quite remarkable feat. I had a 36-hour leave pass commencing at 12 noon on Saturday. We arrived back in barracks after the aforementioned 20-mile march at 11:30hrs. I changed out of my muddy, damp battledress into my spare uniform suit, gathered together the minimum permitted kit, collected my pass from the Orderly Room and walked into Richmond (about 3 miles) where I then caught the train to Darlington. From Darlington I mounted a train to York where I caught a connection for Leeds. By now it was late evening and I managed to catch the last train from Leeds to Manchester which deposited me at Stalybridge railway station at about midnight.

There was of course no available public transport—the bus services had ended very early in wartime, so I walked from Stalybridge to Gee Cross, Hyde (about 6 miles, mainly uphill) where my parents were waiting up for me, arriving at about 2 a.m. Sunday. We sat together talking until about 4 a.m. It was 24 hours since I had paraded at Catterick and since then I had walked over 30 miles with heavy kit. I climbed out of bed at 9 a.m and after eating breakfast visited my grandparents and uncle, ate a hearty traditional Sunday lunch and at 2pm left for Manchester Exchange to catch a series of trains back to Catterick camp, where after delays due to an air raid on York, I arrived at 02:00hrs and crashed into my bed until reveille at 05:45hrs on Monday. It may seem an awful lot of trouble to go to, but I can assure the reader it was worth all the effort it took to get home to my family if only for a visit of a few hours. How we take the ordinary things for granted until we no longer have them.

★★★★★★

Once more back into the business of becoming functioning tank soldiers we fell into a routine of intensive training and long working days. In the course of it all we were taught how to drive a number of different vehicles including lorries and trucks, tanks, Bren gun carriers and tracked armoured personnel carriers.

We were introduced to the wonders of wireless operation, (a fascination for which has stayed with me), and we learned to fire all manner of weapons including pistols (a tank man's personal side-arm), rifles, Bren guns, Tommy guns, Browning and Besa belt-fed heavy machine guns together with the two and six-pounder guns of the tanks themselves.

Without doubt my favourite subject was the wireless and so I was delighted to qualify as a Driver/Operator which meant that my principal job in the tank would be as its wireless operator.

Once off duty there was not a wide choice of entertainment at Catterick. The camp had a Sandy's Home which offered refreshment and games, a NAAFI (Navy, Army and Air Force Institute) canteen, YMCA, etc., and a garrison theatre where on one notable Sunday evening we were able to hear the well-known Joe Loss and his big band in concert. We sometimes walked into Richmond and a popular venue for us there was a large amusement centre which contained various fairground rides, dodgem cars and fruit slot machines. Most attractively we could also cast our young lustful eyes over the cream of Richmond's female talent. Nothing much came of that particular pass time beyond wishful thinking, unfortunately.

My recommendation for officer suitability which had been made after training in Beverley now caught up with me and I was notified that I would be called before a selection board in the near future. In the meantime, it was decided that as potential officer material I should give some ABCA lectures to the troops.

These lectures, sponsored by the Army Bureau of Current Affairs, were designed to educate the troops and to inform them of current thinking regarding the post-war world. These riveting monologues were usually presented by officers in mess rooms during the working day and were widely regarded as extremely worthwhile initiatives, offering as they did the opportunity to smoke with the benefit of official sanction and also to allow one to surreptitiously catch up on a little lost sleep.

It was, therefore, with understandable alarm that I discovered that the lectures I had been nominated to deliver were to be scheduled during soldiers 'free-time' notably after tea on Friday evenings in their own barrack rooms. Furthermore, no officer or NCO was to be present as a pacifying influence whilst I performed this unwelcome duty should the need for one arise. Soldiers did not get much leisure time in training regiments as one may imagine and so what free time they are allowed is understandably considered to be quite precious to them.

I speculated gloomily on the probable reaction of my peers which was about to come in my direction given I would be invading the privacy of their barrack rooms after duties had ceased on a Friday night, of all nights—the night for going into or on the town. Thankfully, as it transpired, when the time came for me to make my debut as a lecturer my audience was, to no small relief on my part, very tolerant of me. I delivered the lectures crisply and as briefly as possible and concluded in the customary way by enquiring if there any questions. To nobody's great astonishment there were none forthcoming so I thanked the assembled ranks (heartfelt in my case) and escaped into the night.

Eventually my summons to the WOSB (War Office Selection Board) arrived. I was to report to a country house (exactly where, I forget after this passage of time) on the following Friday, where I would undergo various tests to determine if I was to become an officer over the weekend and which would conclude on the Sunday evening.

Irrespective of the fact that I was present at this country house to be examined, the experience was, nevertheless, one to be savoured by anyone with my recent history. For the first time since I joined the army I slept between clean white sheets and was served excellent meals at a polished mahogany table by mess waiters.

No one (officially) knew our status as we each wore a cloth band on the upper sleeves of our battledress to conceal any badges of rank. This weekend passed pleasantly enough as we engaged in assault courses, simulated attacks and defensive actions. We took out patrols during which each prospective officer took his turn to command a platoon. Back at the country house there were debates, ink-blot and other psychological tests. Over all, I felt that I had been given a fair examination and so determined to be content with the decision of the selection board, whatever it might be.

Once I had returned to the training regiment, within a couple of days I was called to the Orderly Room and was informed that I had been judged 'unready for a commission at this time. Perhaps having gained a little more experience I would care to apply again.'

Since I had not applied for a commission in the first place I decided that I would follow the golden rule of the army to 'never volunteer for anything' and so I determined to complete my military service in the ranks.

However, now I was separated from my former comrades and stuck in a kind of limbo. Whilst I had been held back pending the WOSB examination and decision, the squad to which I had belonged had been posted away far and wide and so I was placed in a holding squad to await my fate. This squad consisted of the flotsam and jetsam of the camp. Two of its members confided to me that they had managed to actually escape the system. They spent their days in the camp centre YMCA playing snooker and swimming, turning up in any official sense only for meals and pay parades!

★★★★★★

One Sunday I was sent out as part of a regular unit to engage in a mock battle against a Home Guard unit in a scheme designed to hone infantry street fighting skills. This engagement took place in Yarm, near Middlesborough. After being soundly scolded by an irate householder for creeping through his back garden without his permission, I was engaged in a 'shoot-out' with an enthusiastic member of the Home Guard. Each one of us claimed to have killed the other one, and the argument was getting nowhere, but more heated, until it dawned upon me just how ludicrous it was to attempt to establish violent death by means of debate. I immediately conceded the point and agreed with him that I was, indeed, dead by his hand and wandered off to find an umpire. Once found, this official having been informed by me of my inanimate condition, obligingly certified me as a corpse and sent me off to spend the first afternoon of my afterlife contentedly drinking mugs of tea cosseted in the casualty tent.

★★★★★.

Eventually my own posting came through, but any hopes I might have entertained of visiting exotic locations in distant lands were quickly dashed.

I was going nowhere for my posting was to be—of all places—inside Catterick Camp!

CHAPTER 4

Advancing Slowly–Not Always Carefully

My new unit was to be the 110th Regiment, Royal Armoured Corps, otherwise known as the 5th Battalion, The Border Regiment which was of part of the 77th Division, the shoulder flash of which portrayed the legendary King Arthur's sword, Excalibur, being held above the waters of the enchanted lake by the phantom hand of the 'lady'. In the typical black humour of the British soldier someone speculated this was a portent that we might all be about to sink beneath the waters for the final time. Many a true word, as the saying goes, is said in jest.

Half a dozen of us were deposited with full kit by a 15cwt truck at the Orderly Room of our new unit, where our welcome could scarcely have been less cordial if we had been a draft from Hitler's black uniformed SS storm-troopers.

The 5th Battalion of the Border Regiment had survived the evacuation from Dunkirk in 1940 and after being brought up to full strength again had been converted into an armoured unit. It soon became apparent that this change in the regiment's status and function was a thoroughly unpopular and unwelcome one by all concerned. In short, they hated tanks and all their works. So unsurprisingly they reserved an especial dislike for specialist tank soldiers who had never been anything but tank men. This, of course, absolutely included us. This state of affairs was hardly likely to promote *esprit de corps* and so I can honestly declare that

A Valentine tank Mk II

this was the worse unit in which I ever served. I remain eternally grateful that I was never called upon go into action with it though as it transpired that possibility was academic since this regiment never did go into action as an armoured unit. It was broken up in November, 1943

I was allocated to C Squadron whose officers were offensive, ignorant and incompetent. The NCOs were little better, though a notable exception was the Squadron Sergeant Major, a sensible, gruff but kind-hearted disciplinarian.

This time at Catterick constituted a period of unrelieved misery—the weather was perpetually foul, wet and cold, the tanks were Mark I Valentines and 'clapped-out' so our activities were restricted to endless 'schemes' on muddy tank training grounds.

★★★★★★

The Valentine tank was made by Vickers-Armstrong and had been in service since the summer of 1941. The idea behind the design of the Valentine was to try to combine the lower weight of a cruiser tank with the heavier armour of an infantry tank. It had a two pounder gun in a two-man turret and low silhouette which meant it was a smaller vehicle with a cramped interior for its crew. The end result produced a lighter tank with less heavy armour than the Matilda infantry tank though it could produce about the same turn of speed. One of the most significant consequences of this design was that the crew commander had not only his own job to attend to, but also had to be personally involved with the operation of the gun. How that would bear on my own experiences with the Valentine before long, the reader will discover in due course.

★★★★★★

It is worth mentioning that one of the more commendable aspects of my new regiment was that it possessed a first class rugby football fifteen, reputed to be second only to the legendary Royal Corps of Signals, Catterick team which dominated services rugby at that time.

To maintain our team's morale and demonstrate the regiment's solidarity with them, the Commanding Officer decreed

A Valentine tank Mk III

that everyone not attending the Saturday afternoon rugby matches in which the regimental team would be engaged would be required instead to spend two hours developing his personal fitness on the assault course. As one might imagine, the turn-out of enthusiastic and highly incentivised ruby supporters among our ranks made for an impressive spectacle as we all marched in a solid body to the sports-ground, led on by stirring airs played by a solitary regimental piper.

******

In the early spring, 1943, the regiment had a stroke of luck which removed us from the constrictive environments of the camp at Catterick. This came in the form of a move (all be it not so very far) to Otley, Yorkshire. We were stationed there in Nissen huts in Farnley Park, a local beauty spot in the shadow of the impressive Chevin ridge. We shared the area with the other two regiments in our brigade, The Manchester Regiment and the King's Own (Liverpool) Regiment. We had little to do with them socially, as their quarters were rather remote from ours which was just as well from our perspective considering that these two regiments were for some reason engaged in a constant state of feuding with each other.

Fights between the men of Manchesters and those of the King's Own were commonplace and I think the men of The Border Regiment demonstrated a collective and conspicuous wisdom on this occasion to ensure they never became embroiled in these altercations or indeed in the greater quarrel-whatever it was about. On reflection the dispute may well have been no more complicated than the issues inherent in placing 'Manchester' in close proximity to 'Liverpool'.

One could have no complaints about the area in which we now resided for it was among picturesque north of England countryside. The town of Otley was also quite attractive and our own billets a considerable improvement on those we occupied in Catterick. The weather, too, improved and I actually enjoyed several exercises in the rolling countryside of the Yorkshire Dales.

At the end of May came significant news, we were given

14 days' embarkation leave which meant, of course, that before long I was about to find myself considerably closer to the war than I had been thus far as a soldier. The 110th Regiment, RAC, regiment was now a holding unit tasked with supplying drafts for overseas. I spent my leave conscientiously visiting practically every friend and relation I possessed, the underlying motivation for the thorough manner in which was undertaken being, it has to be admitted, that there was a possibility I might not return and so this would be the last any of them saw of me. I wondered if I was alone in finding this duty rather depressing in practice as well as in theory.

★★★★★★

On returning to the regiment at about 22.00hrs on the Sunday evening after this leave ended, I looked at Squadron Orders board and read that a big 'scheme' was planned for the following day and that I was to drive the 1st Troop Leader's tank. This came as a considerable surprise to me as I had been exclusively employed as a wireless operator up to this point and my driving skills, such as they were, had suffered from a lack of practice

I protested my case to be excused this duty in vain and so the following morning with some trepidation I collected my tank which bore the appellation 'Blind Tarn' upon its hull.

★★★★★★

All tanks were given names, a practice for vehicles which long pre-dated the time when the now famous British logistics company, Eddie Stobart adopted it for their fleet of vehicles. Our tanks bore names, understandably enough given the regiment's origins, associated with the northern county of Cumbria. Blind Tarn, incidentally, is the name given to one particular sheet of water cradled in the hills of the English Lake District which is distinctive because no source to fill it is visible and no stream escapes it. Romantics might regard this feature as a small and beautiful lake, whilst pragmatists might refer to it as a very large puddle though deep enough to drown in. To me it was the name painted on the flank of a memorably problematic Valentine tank, so I stand with the pragmatists.

★★★★★★

I climbed aboard, started the engine and drove the tank back to the departure point to meet my crew. I always found the Valentine tank an absolute 'pig' to drive and this one was clearly not going to prove to be an exception to the rule.

To begin with it required the skills of a contortionist to get into the driving seat. In most tanks you drop through a hatch on to the seat, but the Valentine had side flaps or doors, rather like the ill-fated De Lorean sports car's famous 'gull-wings'. The way to get in to this tank was to insert the feet first and holding on to the frame, wriggle about until the whole body could be contrived into its bowels.

The seat was rudimentary—a thin cushion on the chequer-plated floor. In effect, the driver sat with his legs stretched out in front of him, the body forming an 'L' shape. The clutch consisted of a metal bar suspended pendulum-fashion while the footbrake and accelerator were configured in a conventional position.

The tank was steered by two levers, rising from the floor and with ratchet pistol grips to lock them into position. If one pulled on the left stick and the tank turned left; pulling on the right stick caused the tank to turn right. When both sticks were pulled back simultaneously and the tank stopped dead.

Pulling back on a stick applied a brake to a driving sprocket on that side. Because the drive went through a differential the other driving sprocket went correspondingly faster; consequently, the tank pivoted on the slower or stationary track and the turn was made.

The only visibility for the driver was through a narrow slit protected by armoured glass. The effect was similar to looking through a letter box. There was no peripheral vision—only the area directly in front of the tank and about 20 yards ahead was within the field of view. It followed that the driver needed a considerable amount of guidance from the crew commander concerning when to make a turn and the degree of turn necessary. This was communicated to the driver through the intercom.

We moved off and everything went without a hitch for the

first few miles. I found the gears very stiff to operate—the gear lever operated through a gate and third gear required both hands to force it in!

Eventually we came to a village and entered it. At the end of the main street was a public house. I could see the sign in front of the building and a scattering of benches outside. We appeared to be heading straight for it all. No message to change direction came through my intercom—was the crew commander asleep or had the communication equipment malfunctioned? I lost my nerve so at about 15 yards from the public house I pulled on the left stick. There was a tortured scream from the turret—no need for the intercom this time, I heard him well enough! Filtering out the expletives I gathered from the commander that I was required to steer right and continue to head for the public house until ordered to do otherwise. I had committed a cardinal sin of tank driving which was manoeuvring without orders. The lieutenant blistered my ears with threats of what he would do to me if I ever deviated from a direction ordered by him so much as an inch without his permission in the future.

Having been thus suitably chastised and having been given my new course, we continued to our ultimate destination, a vehicle harbour on the moors which was to be our base for the next three days. There was no doubt the crew commander was in the right to admonish me because I should have trusted his judgement but, unreasonably on my part I suppose, the reprimand I had received from this officer rankled my dignity.

After a quick break for sandwiches, the 'scheme' started. We were fired upon by smoke mortars and upon the order (one must, of course, wait for one of those) the tanks began their advance. After about a hundred yards I spotted, directly ahead of us, a huge crater, about ten feet wide and six feet deep. Common sense demanded someone took evasive action, but no command to do so came to my ear from above.

The events of a few hours earlier came back into my mind and brewed there wickedly. Right, I decided—if no orders came to the contrary, I would drive us straight into this hole. Still no word concerning large pits, one way or the other, came through the intercom.

My commander was obviously distracted by the 'battle' going on all around us and completely failed to notice where we were going. The tank continued on its way. I felt the front end of the tank fall away as the tracks sought purchase in clear air and I gripped the sticks tightly, anchoring myself firmly into the driving seat. We pitched forward and down and yet further down we went. Suddenly there was the most enormous crash, jarring every bone in my body, followed by a cascade of sundry objects dropping from every crevice of the turret. Howls of anguish and pain from elsewhere were followed by colourful curses and then by a silence.

Sweet revenge had been taken and honour satisfied.

Fortunately, no one was hurt; the wireless operator and gunner had anticipated the impact when they felt the front end go light and even my chum, the commander, was only shaken. He was however, considerably miffed, casting aspersions on both my eyesight and my mental acuity. Tongue in cheek, I explained that I had been waiting for his orders as, for all I could know, he may have been intending to put us into the hole to take cover. He gave me a most peculiar look following this 'innocent' rationale, but I think he appreciated there was nothing he could do to me irrespective of what he suspected was really behind what had happened.

At any rate, we had the bonus of a cushy two days before ahead with little onerous to occupy us. The tank had to be towed out because the suspension was wrecked and the consequential repair work upon it lasted for the duration of the 'scheme'.

We went on from this exercise to the town of Harrogate where our tanks formed part of a display for a 'war chest' collection day. We spent a pleasant day entertaining children and nurses from a nearby hospital and allowing them to clamber all over the tanks, inside and out.

Leaving the field, I snapped a track in the soft earth and after repairing this breakage, we had only travelled a couple of miles when I found myself stuck in second gear. The fitters discovered that the selector forks in the gear box had broken and so we were faced with a very pedestrian night drive from Harrogate to Otley trundling along in this low gear. The fitter sergeant decided that he would drive the tank to nurse the engine, although by this time I think he considered me accident-prone so this would be the safest course of action. My friend, the lieutenant, announced that he would clean the two-pounder gun as we went along to save time instead of doing it on the following day, while I, in his stead, acted as crew commander.

So we rumbled slowly through the night. My troop leader's efforts with the gun suffered something of a setback when he dropped a vital pin from the breech block into the innards of the tank where it disappeared from view with no hope of its recovery in any immediate future. His response to this blunder was to tie up the remaining bits of gun mechanism in a cloth and suspend it from the barrel where it hung as a conspicuous signal that all was not well.

At 23:00hrs, back at camp, I finally parked 'Blind Tarn' in the compound. Four days earlier, I had taken out a perfectly serviceable Valentine. I now handed back a tank with a gearbox no longer fit for purpose ('demic' as we would say), a gun with a vital part missing from it (though not missing from the tank since it was somewhere inside it) and an armoured vehicle with a somewhat traumatised suspension.

It crossed my mind at that point that surely soldiers had been sent to the courts martial for lesser transgressions and the responsibility for all of this damage had the potential to land on my shoulders. I went to bed that night in very apprehensive frame of mind and remained in that unsettling condition for several days following. To my surprise and relief though, I never heard any more about it.

★★★★★★

During the next week several of us who had come from the 51st Training Regiment discovered that we were owed another week of leave. The Squadron Sergeant Major concurred with this verdict and promptly sent us off to enjoy it.

When I arrived back home out of the blue so soon after my recent departure it caused my family some consternation and confusion. I had already said my emotional goodbyes at the end my actual embarkation leave and yet here I was back again only a week later even though my protracted absence had been reliably forecast. My parents were delighted to see me, of course, under any circumstances, but I am sure my mother secretly harboured concerns that I might have deserted.

Extra leave was quickly over and back with the regiment once again, we spent a final week being kitted out with new headgear in the form of solar topees and other tropical climate gear and submitting to the needles of our final inoculations.

We had one day of freedom in Otley to do some final shopping and we then were off on our way.

We entrained late afternoon on a Tuesday and in the middle of the night arrived, *via* Edinburgh Waverley at Gourock on the Clyde in Scotland where we boarded a troopship, the SS *Santa Rosa*.

This was it at last—we really were heading off to fight the enemy.

CHAPTER 5

Over Sea and Sand

Our ship, the *Santa Rosa*, was an American vessel, one of four identical sainted sisters, built in 1930 as a passenger and cargo liner for the Grace Line and which, in her heyday, had elegantly cruised the route between the east to west coasts of the United States *via* the Caribbean and its islands then onwards through the Panama Canal before turning northwards again. In her civilian livery she was considered to be something of a beauty with winged twin funnels, a sweeping bow and long lines suggestive it was said of 'speed, luxury and moonlit tropical nights'. There were those who could still see the romance in her even when she was painted in her wartime grey, but it took more imagination than most of her military passengers could summon that April in 1943 to appreciate what charms she might have hidden beneath her drab overalls. To the soldiers who crammed aboard her then she was just a typical troopship and of necessity very crowded and uncomfortable. The lady had definitely come down in the world.

That said, the food was plentiful and good, although the breakfasts took some getting used to. Having spam or bacon, scrambled egg, baked beans, hash browns, jam and waffles all served on the same plate, and sometimes on top of each other gave our taste buds a mountain to climb.

Our course took us southwards. The Bay of Biscay, sometimes notorious for its stormy waves, was on its best behaviour as we progressed over its untroubled waters and the weather was sunny and warm. There were some cases of sea sickness on board, but there are some people who will get motion sickness on a boating lake.

Apart from sessions of daily PT, we spent our time reading, writing letters and lying about on deck in the sunshine. There were the occasional obligatory lifeboat drills, during which I invariably got lost, and a couple of alerts that warned of the potential presence of prowling U-boats in our area. Apart from those diverting entertainments our own cruise into the Mediterranean Sea was more or less uneventful.

Then, at last, one morning as we emerged on deck we could see the North African coast with the city of Algiers sparkling in the early morning sunlight. It was my first glimpse of 'abroad' and very impressive it was since this was a place the like of which I had never seen before. The multi-coloured, but predominantly white buildings in the square architecture of the Arabs rose up from the waterfront and were a magnificent sight to me since the place also emanated all the sounds and smells of a culture which was totally alien to anything I had known. I, unfortunately, did not get to see more of Algiers than these tantalising glimpses. The first sight of Africa is not just a view into another country or yet another continent, it is to look upon another world. We were only there for a short time to embark more troops and a few hours after we had docked at the quayside we cast off and were once more on our way.

★★★★★★

Our actual destination was the port of Philippeville further to the east on the Algerian coast, a place that appeared to be far less impressive than Algiers. The town was named by the French in the middle of the nineteenth century hence its distinctly European sounding name though, as with most places in this part of the Mediterranean, it had existed as a port from ancient times. Peoples throughout history come and go and with their passing the names of the towns they created change. The Romans apparently called it Rusicade, to us passing through it was Philippeville. Following the departure of the French from their colonies in North Africa

SANTA *ROSA* AS A TROOPSHIP

the town once again became an Arabic one and these days it is called Skikda. History like this should have a tendency to put the squabbles of nations in some perspective.

★★★★★★

We disembarked from our troopship in the middle of the afternoon and after forming up on the quayside saw our kit-bags and large packs loaded on to lorries. In all probability all the men who were carried on the *Santa Rosa* during wartime thought that they had seen the last of her, but that was possibly not so. Her final performance was in the motion picture, *Raise the Titanic* made in 1978, when she was used as a set to represent the interiors and bows of the doomed cruise liner. So some of her former passengers may have seen her again on the screen without ever recognising her.

We were marched off to a transit camp arriving after a couple hours at a tented area where we dumped the balance of our kit, were fed a quick meal and settled down for the night.

The next two or three days were taken up with parades, the filling in of documentation, eating and, in our leisure time, visiting the camp cinema. Day by day our numbers dwindled as men disappeared on various postings and though I knew my turn would come around soon enough, I had no idea where I would be going at this point.

On one Friday night I went to bed in my bivouac at nightfall, only to wake up an hour later feeling dreadfully ill. I was burning hot and assailed at both ends of my person simultaneously by the most violent vomiting and diarrhoea. By 08:00hrs on Saturday morning I was feeling no better, but was able to get up from my bed, dress myself and stagger off to report sick.

The Medical Officer examined me and my condition was diagnosed as enteric fever. The fact that this was a far from uncommon condition to befall those who step onto the sands of anywhere in North Africa did not help me to feel any better about it for it drains a body physically, mentally and quite literally. He advised me to go straight back to bed and stay there until Monday, drinking only water, until he saw me again on the sick parade. This seemed like an excellent suggestion to me so I staggered back to my tent, pausing only to fill up my water bottle from the water point, collapsed into bed and promptly fell asleep.

I was awakened by the intrusive voice of the orderly corporal.

"Trooper Knowles? Found you at last!" he chirruped with nauseating cheerfulness, "Got news for you, mate—you're posted. 16th/5th Lancers. Hurry up and get your kit together, the truck leaves at 14:30hrs"

I blearily looked at my watch which told me it was already 14:00hrs. This was not welcome news.

"But I'm sick, Corp," I groaned, "The M.O says I have enteric lever and I have to stay in bed until Monday."

"Sorry about that, mate," he replied, "but you're posted. Report sick at the other end."

I had been in the army for a year at this point which was long enough to know that there was no point looking for sympathy or arguing my case. He had his orders, and he was not about to go looking for the M.O to verify my story. There was nothing else for it—I had to get up and go.

Feeling like the walking dead, I gathered my kit and struggled over to the Orderly Room where an open-backed 3-tonne truck awaited. There were already about half a dozen other black-bereted unfortunates aboard it, their evident good health and general state of fitness serving to make me feel even lower in spirits.

I heaved myself up over the tailboard, scrambled on board and almost immediately we were on our way. There were no seats in this conveyance, of course. We stood, holding on to whatever supports we could find, whilst our 3-tonner, open to the mid-afternoon African heat bumped and jolted its way over the 20 or so miles of uneven road. The effect all this had on me, given my condition, requires no elaboration.

Eventually, we turned off down a dirt track between the villages of Robertville and Sidi Medrich, just outside of which, in an olive grove amid the sand which stretched uphill on both sides of a narrow valley, I first beheld 'B' Squadron, 16th/5th Lancers.

This unit was destined to be my home and my family for the following four years.

CHAPTER 6

Scarlet Lancer-Occasionally Purple

The following morning all of the most recent arrived draft were interviewed individually by Major Gill, Officer Commanding, 'B' Squadron, 16th/5th Lancers. In marked contrast to my reception when I joined The Border Regiment I was made to feel welcome among the lancers and in spite of my lingering illness I felt that things had taken a decided turn for the better for me.

The regiment, along with the rest of 26th Armoured Brigade had seen some hard fighting in Tunisia, had taken casualties and it was those vacancies we were there to fill.

★★★★★★

The regiment was in India when the war broke out and returned to the UK in 1940 becoming a constituent part of the 26th Armoured Brigade within the 6th Armoured Division. The 26th Armoured Brigade consisted of the 16th/5th Lancers, 17th/21st Lancers, 2nd Lothians and Border Horse, the 4th Queen's Hussars, 10th Battalion Rifle Brigade and the 1st Battalion King's Royal Rifle Corps.

The 6th Armoured Division had taken part in 'Operation Torch' in November 1942 which was the invasion of French North Africa (Morocco and Tunisia). The division first saw action as part of V Corps of the British First Army in the Tunisian Campaign and was engaged in the run for Tunis and the hard fought Battle for the Kasserine Pass.

★★★★★★

I was allocated to 2nd Troop, commanded by Lieutenant H.A.G Brooke who was, in the fullness of time, destined to become colonel of the regiment. For the present, however, he commanded a tank troop almost devoid of the essential ingredient of actual tanks, since at that time the squadron only had one tank—a Sherman—to call its own. Gradually, replacement tanks were received and we were able to commence work on them to make them ready for action

★★★★★★

These new tanks were also American made Shermans which carried a 75mm gun and which ran on diesel fuel. The M4 Sherman medium tank was the work-horse of the American and British armies during the Second World War and was manufactured in large quantities. It was cheap to produce and comparatively reliable though in the event of a breakdown it was also straightforward to repair and maintain. During the early years of the conflict the Sherman stood up quite well in armour and weaponry against its German opposing armoured vehicles of similar type. The subsequent development of heavier tanks by the Germans reversed its individual fortunes later in the war in this respect, though it retained the advantage of being available for battlefield use in far greater numbers than its rivals.

★★★★★★

I never did report sick, and remarkably my enteric fever cleared up after a few days. The weather was superb, as one would expect of North Africa, but one had to adjust to the special requirements of living in the very dry and often hot country.

We slept under mosquito nets with a piece of canvas or tarpaulin rigged up from the nearest tree to offer shade. Often I slept in the open. The regular adherence to anti-malarial precautions was taken very seriously. We were issued with a dose of Mepacrin tablets daily and anyone found sleeping without the covering of a mosquito net was for the 'high jump'. One of our corporals, in fact, was reduced to the ranks for this offence.

During the daytime the heat was enervating. I can remember wondering at times whether I could summon up enough en-

SHERMAN TANKS OF THE REGIMENT BEING USED IN ACTION FOR THE FIRST TIME DURING THE ADVANCE TO THE KASSERINE PASS—25TH FEBRUARY 1943

ergy to go to the cookhouse for the midday meal.

We quickly learned not to put our bare hands on the metal exterior of the tank as painful blistering could be the result. The ground was pulverised into dust which lay about six inches deep, a light, almost golden colour which had the appearance of the desert sand. It found a way into everywhere and into everything including us. We had dust in our hair, in our ears, up our noses, in every fold and seam of our clothes, in and on the food we food ate, and in our mouths whether we were chewing on it in one form or another or not. A limited amount of drinking water was available, also plenty of 'non-potable' water to wash with, and I contrived at least one 'bath' per day, standing alongside the contents of a sawn-off oil drum.

The other great nuisance was the omnipresence of flies. They crawled, flew and buzzed all over us perpetually from sunrise to sunset. Every exposed part of the body quickly harboured its quota of these pestilential horrors; they clustered around the mouth and upon every forkful of food which had to be cleared of them before being hurriedly shovelled put into the mouth. Any slight cut or sore one incurred attracted them and often these abrasions developed into the dreaded desert sores which were then treated with gentian violet anti-fungal dye. The unfortunate recipient of this remedy thus painted then had to live for weeks with garish purple blotches adorning his face, neck and other exposed parts, which was most embarrassing when walking out on day leave to Philippeville. The prospect of wandering around the town decorated like some colour variant of a woad-adorned Ancient Briton, understandably, did nothing for one's self-confidence.

To cap it all I contracted impetigo which manifested itself by covering my entire face and neck with suppurating scabs. To avoid making this appalling condition worse, I decided not to shave. However, when I reported sick, the Medical Officer, a liverish individual with a perpetual hangover, metaphorically 'hit the (tent) roof'.

How dare I, he shrieked, sully his sick parade and medical

inspection room looking like a tramp! I was to go back to my quarters immediately, shave and be quick about it before daring to return to his presence. Fuming, I stomped back to the squadron lines, got out my razor, lathered and attacked my face with such ferocity that every sore was brutally decapitated. I represented myself to the M.O literally dripping with blood. My face looked as though it had been flayed. Surely he would now, I thought, see the error of his ways! Sadly, he made no comment—contrition from officers not being commonplace as it regarded the other ranks. However, instead of applying the usual gentian violet dye treatment, he proposed to treat me with a new ointment which, he forecast, would clear up the condition in about five days. This remedy turned out to be a vast improvement on being daubed with purple war-paint and, as it transpired, actually worked. So the experience was not all bad since at least he did his job properly.

★★★★★★

Whether my experience was unique I do not know, but during my five years of service I found British and Irish Medical Officers and Roman Catholic *padres* to be invariably foul-tempered and immensely unsympathetic. Fortunately, I seldom had any need to be in contact with any of them. By contrast, the most unstuffy, un-regimental, practical and pleasant of these types were South African Medical Officers and Church of England *padres*. Possibly, in my case, it was just the luck of the draw. One can only take people, as the saying goes, as one finds them.

★★★★★★

Perhaps unsurprisingly given where we were, thirst was a great and perpetual problem for everyone. The heat rapidly dehydrated us and we could never seem to get enough to drink. I was teetotal at this point so any drinkable liquid was principally just a quencher of eternal thirst so far as I was concerned. So when someone turned up with a supply of Algerian red wine at 6d per mess-tin, I eagerly bought some, though I cannot speak for the motives of everyone who did so. Since I had never taken alcohol before and was possessed of a great thirst I downed two full mess-tins of it in short order. I suspect a number of my peers were no more worldly wise than I was, for the next morning several of us woke up in peculiar places without any recollection of how we had managed to arrive in them. The experience was not repeated.

Work consisted of the usual elements with which I was familiar, but now tempered by the benefits of the squadron's actual battle experiences in Tunisia. Theoretical speculation had gone forever from this unit. Training was, we newcomers knew well, conducted by people who had experienced war at first hand and with the prospect of more of the same to come before long, those of us who were tyros were disposed to listen carefully and learn well. Interestingly enough, when we first arrived with the lancers we were told by our new colleagues that our journey to join them had been a waste of time as the regiment was scheduled to return to the UK in the near future to prepare for the invasion of Europe. Whether there was any truth in these rumours I never discovered, but following the allied landings in Sicily we heard no more of them.

★★★★★★

During August we 'new boys' were taken out on driving instruction. Each unit in the army, no doubt in possession of ample bitter experience to support the wisdom of this unwritten policy, never believes that its unproven soldiers have accomplished the skills that they claim to possess. In consequence every new arrival is reassessed wherever they go. It is tedious to have one's *bona fides* questioned, but I was not inclined to complain about this evaluation of my abilities since it held all the promise of an enjoyable outing. Our route took us by 15cwt truck to the Algerian city of Constantine. Originally Roman, (and named for the 4th century emperor) Constantine was a place of great antiquity intermingled by the Arabic architecture and influences of later times.

This labyrinth clings precariously to the edge of the precipice on either side of a rocky gorge at the bottom of which, far below, runs the River Rhumel. The chasm which divides the city is spanned by a dramatic, single arch bridge and the appearance of this place is a stunning combination of the ancient world, the mosques and minarets of Islam and a natural landscape at its most spectacular. Constantine is about 60 miles from the Mediterranean coast so this full day session, which was supervised by Sergeant Shuttleworth, was a useful, memorable and much appreciated experience, especially for someone like me who had seen very little of the wider world.

★★★★★★

As a tank soldier, irrespective of all the skills I was required to master, my abiding interest remained in all things concerning wireless. We were fortunate in having some extremely knowledgeable instructors on the subject in the unit and I so learned a great deal about wireless theory which was to prove useful for many years ahead until, in fact, the introduction of transistors and the passing of the vacuum tube which instituted major changes in the development of wireless equipment and much else. The underrated humble transistor, for those who do not know, is reckoned by some authorities to be the most significant development of the 20th century and without its development in the late 1940's and commercial introduction in the mid-1950's, the digital age could not have been developed practically for the many products that are now so familiar and used every day by almost everybody.

I elected to take an upgrade course to improve my knowledge and usefulness and eventually took a test on theory and practical wireless fault-finding. Every examinee was presented with a No. 19 wireless set to work upon which had been previously modified so that it produced several faults. The candidate then had to trace and repair the faults and deliver a summary of the logic which led to his diagnosis. I achieved, if my memory serves me well, a P1, which elevated me to instructor status, but more importantly it brought an increase in pay of a shilling a day which went a long way in those days.

★★★★★★

Off duty, in the evening, we would ascend the hill upon

which the NAAFI canteen was sited, there to relax, drink 'char', chew 'wads' and work our way huge slices of watermelon. The mug of 'char' and the fistful of 'wad' were familiar and essential components of what was required necessary to hold every ordinary serviceman's body and soul in concert during this war.

The terms have passed into obscurity for later generations inevitably, but 'char' was, of course, the British soldier's staple beverage, brewed and drunk on every possible occasion—strong and sweet. In fact, it is nothing less than the archetypal English 'cuppa' tea though usually taken in industrially sized portions. The word, 'char', comes the age of empire and the British Raj in India so well known to many British soldiers in times past and, of course, originates in the country where much of this beloved leaf was grown. The genuine article has its own special characteristics generally unable to be exactly replicated outside the sub-continent where it is known by its Hindi name, 'chai'.

The British are infamous for changing foreign language words to roll easily off their own tongues—hence, 'char'. A 'wad' is simpler to define since the name speaks to substance and is a wedge of practically anything of satisfying proportions designed to be readily eaten in the hand from a currant bun, or thickly made sandwich to a hefty piece of cake. I suppose its use by soldiers might date back to the similarity in appearance of these things to the wad used to hold down a charge in muzzle loaded firearms and cannons. Watermelons, as most people know, are tasteless on the whole, but a convenient way to get refreshing liquid inside the body from a more or less solid form, so fairly useful for those who live in proximity to desert-like conditions.

I was engaged one evening in the above described activity when I was fascinated to observe the behaviour of a colony of ants. I was sitting by the side of the anthill and as the light faded, all the ants disappeared down the entrance hole to their underground city. For about a minute everything was deserted, then two ants, red and black in colour, emerged. One turned left, the other turned right and they began a series of patrols around the perimeter, meeting halfway before retracing their beat like tiny six-legged guardsmen. Their performance was so similar to a military sentry duty that I felt a sort of kinship with them. It is peculiar how the small things can stick in the mind.

★★★★★★

By this time, I had formed a friendship with a fellow new-comer to the regiment whose name was John Hart. He was about eight years older than I was and in civilian life had been a foreman carpenter in Folkestone, Kent. Our friendship was to survive the war incidentally, and we remained in contact when he emigrated with his wife to Australia, Fiji and finally to New Zealand. To my regret, we lost touch with each other in the 1970's. John was in HQ Troop and as our opportunities for so-cialising were restricted since we were in different troops, he suggested that I apply for a transfer to his troop. This hop was achieved without difficulty and I moved my kit across to the HQ area.

★★★★★★

During this time, we were involved in training exercises with the battalions of the 201st Guards Motor Brigade. This infantry brigade was comprised of elements of The Coldstream Guards, The Scots Guards, The Rifle Brigade, The Grenadier Guards, The Irish Guards and the Welsh Guards. By the time we were working with this brigade it had already seen much heavy cam-paigning in North Africa and, in fact, this unit was a reformation of the 201st Guards Brigade which had eventually been com-pelled to surrender in Tobruk in July, 1942.

★★★★★★

In July the heat was horrendous to endure, reaching at its most fearsome 112 degrees Fahrenheit. Of course these temper-atures were not just insufferable for human beings, they also had the effect of making the landscape and everything in it tinder dry. Predictably, this combustible material could be ignited into a quickly spreading conflagration by the encouragement of the tiniest spark. This phenomenon actually took place during our time in Algeria and we were called out to assist in attempting to contain the ensuing blaze. This proved, to say the least, to be an interesting diversion which involved us spending several days fighting fires which had taken hold in the trees in the country's renowned cork forests. On the last day of this battle against the elements I found myself in some peril, since without my initially noticing it I discovered that I was being speedily encircled by the advancing flames as a result of a sudden change in the direction of the wind. Needless to say the experience gave me quite a fright, but fortunately, I managed to select the right available option for an escape route and all ended well.

★★★★★★

As the summer drew to a close, my friend and I decided to show some initiative as it regarded our own living accommodation and creature comforts. John Hart managed to procure several sheets of corrugated iron and some timber with which he constructed a base for our two-man bivouac.

Under his expert supervision, I laboured to sink six posts in the ground around which we bent and nailed the corrugated iron, leaving a doorway through which to enter. The canvas was then stretched over a timber framework attached to the sides and fastened securely with the guy ropes to pegs in the ground. Inside, he built two beds with a two-foot space in between to enable us to move about. Between the beds at the top was a headboard arrangement which incorporated a bookshelf and a narrow table for mugs of tea and other comforts.

In short, luxury on a scale hitherto undreamed of was now ours! When this palace was finished we hosted the arrival of a stream of visitors, most of whom were lost in admiration at our expertise and achievement though some detractors decried it, claiming they would prefer to stay in their more conventional ground-based tents. These critics, however, were fated to soon revise their opinion on the matter.

One night at the end of October it began to rain. It rained, in fact, as a deluge of near Biblical proportions. All night long we lay in our beds and listened to the cascade of water rushing down the hillside on which our camp was based. Intermingled with the cacophony of this aquatic symphony were the anguished cries of the ground-dwellers whose beds, belongings and even tents were being swept away into the night.

The morning sun brought forth a scene of devastation in our camp area. Almost alone among the dwellings of the squadron which had been standing on the previous day, our tent had survived intact. Furthermore, we noted with some pride, not a drop of water had penetrated inside it to dampen our property or our enthusiasm for the success of our project. The only adjustment required to our home, we realised, was that we needed to dig a drainage ditch around its base.

Obviously the rainy season was upon us and for the next few days we all spent our waking hours digging deep trenches to collect and divert the fallen rain water. It was my first experience of digging trenches, though one which was to be repeated *ad infinitum* later on in my war.

So this situation provided us with invaluable practice in manual excavation and it was here that I learned the secret of extended periods of digging which is to resist the temptation to set too fast a pace in an enthusiasm to see the job quickly concluded. This error of judgement will guarantee that one's energy and resolve will inevitably soon flag. Select and set, instead, a rate of activity which one can confidently maintain for hour after hour and the task becomes an easy one.

Soon the whole camp area was covered in a network of waterways, which were defined by lines of white tape, which prompted the circulation of a gem of army argot which I have taken the liberty of extracting from one particular squadron's orders. It read, in all seriousness, as follows:

> The drainage trenches in the squadron area have now been clearly marked by white tapes and the practice of falling into these trenches during the hours of darkness will cease forthwith.

★★★★★★

In the spirit of cordiality which resulted from our cooperation with the Guards Motor Brigade in the recent joint exercises, the lancers had exchanged visits with the 3rd Battalion,

Grenadier Guards. To our surprise and delight their commanding officer subsequently invited the whole of our regiment to stay with his battalion for Christmas and the New Year. The guardsmen were stationed at Constantine and we were to stay with them for almost a fortnight. We left our own camp on the 22nd of December and were soon comfortably settled into to our temporary quarters. Unfortunately, the weather was truly awful being perpetually wet and cold, but the planned entertainment for us all went ahead irrespective of this drawback.

On Christmas Eve there was a football match played between guards and lancers which the guards won. After a church service on Christmas Day, both units marched through Constantine led by the band of the Grenadiers playing in the fine style for which they are justifiably famous. The day ended with a splendid dinner for everyone followed by what seemed to be an innumerable number of toasts in which the sentiments expressed covered every element of goodwill that could be brought to the minds of both parties.

The following day, traditionally Boxing Day to the British wherever they happened to be, dawned with the weather promising to be fine and we went to a race meeting at the Sidi Mabrouk racecourse. The following two days were occupied by a cross-country race (which I am pleased to report I managed to avoid), a treasure hunt (in which I was unsuccessful in the finding of any treasure) and a musical concert which was far less demanding, and thus more diverting, than either of the afore mentioned as far as actual entertainment value was concerned. The rest of our holiday consisted of combined training, which was actually more enjoyable than it sounds as though it has the potential to be.

By the time all the festivities had concluded the weather had turned for the worse again and the new year of 1944 arrived in Algeria with a chill in the air and a downpour of rain. It was still raining as the regiment bid its farewells to its guardsmen friends, packed up its gear and on January 3rd departed for Robertville.

'*Out with old and in with the new*', as the popular turn of the year saying goes is generally meant to imply that the future holds the potential promise of brighter days ahead. Whether they would be brighter for all of us was unlikely, but changes certainly were imminently in the offing for the men of the 16th/5th Lancers. We were very soon to depart from the shores of North Africa. The war was entering its fifth dark year and though to this point I had seen little of it, that too was about to change because we were now about to be inexorably drawn towards fields where battles were raging.

CHAPTER 7

A Journey into Battle

At about midnight on the 5th of January, 1944, the 16th/5th Lancers was put on notice with immediate effect to move to the Italian theatre of war and so an advance party forthwith flew to Naples to make preparations for our arrival in force.

★★★★★★

Whilst it is well known that at company or squadron level an ordinary soldier's understanding of what is going on day to day is defined by what he has been told should happen and is happening combined with what he can see happening in front of his nose, we knew of course, that our regiment was not among the first Allied troops to set foot on Italian soil, so our activities would not embrace the entire story of the campaign in Italy.

The Allied armies had invaded the island of Sicily some six months previously in July, 1943. German and Italian forces were compelled to give up the island six weeks later. Montgomery and the 8th Army moved onto the 'toe' of the Italian 'boot' in early September and within a week the Italian forces had agreed to an armistice. Mussolini's rule effectively came to an end which came as little surprise to the Germans since they expected they would need to defend the Italian mainland alone. Most Italian forces were disarmed, the Fascist government of Italy died and the majority of Italian citizens did not mourn its passing.

American and British forces effected amphibious landings at Salerno and Taranto on the western coast of the Italian mainland in the hope that this would force the Germans precipitously northward. Instead they responded with typical well considered, pre-planned tactical expertise and dogged resistance. Stubborn defence and begrudging retreat by German forces became the order of the conflict. By January 1944, German forces were firmly established behind the defensive lines which stretched, coast to coast, from the Tyrrhenian Sea to the Adriatic Sea. Field-Marshal Kesselring had sagely counselled Hitler to fight the campaign in Italy as far away from the borders of the Fatherland as possible. These so called 'Winter Lines', established at their western end just north of Naples, were the first barrier that demanded to be purchased in blood by the Allies. They would not be the last bitterly contested obstacle in this campaign and these phenomenal defences by brave men would have made legends of them were they not held in the name of a rotten and corrupt cause. So it was that the laurels concerning them rightly went to those who fought, were mangled or died to break through them.

From this point in this book that is the story of the British Army in Italy until the Spring of 1945. It is the story of the 16th/5th Lancers which was the regiment I am proud to call my own and so, at last, it is my own story—the personal account of one young soldier in a tank regiment at the sharp end of war.

★★★★★★

On the 8th of January, 1944, in the early afternoon, the regiment moved to the dockside at Philippeville. At 16:00hrs we began loading everything we possessed from the Sherman tanks to the tool-boxes and by 21:30hrs everything was stowed and ready to go.

All that was 'B' Squadron, 16th/5th Lancers was gathered together on one LST (Landing Ship, Tank) floating on the blue Mediterranean ready to sail northwards to Italy. As usual, living conditions were typically very cramped, but this was a new experience and we enjoyed the change of scene. Our navy hosts were amiable and during the voyage we paid several visits to the crew's quarters for a chat. On the 10th we set sail. A convoy was assembled consisting of fifteen LSTs protected by an escort of three American warships. Moving along the North African

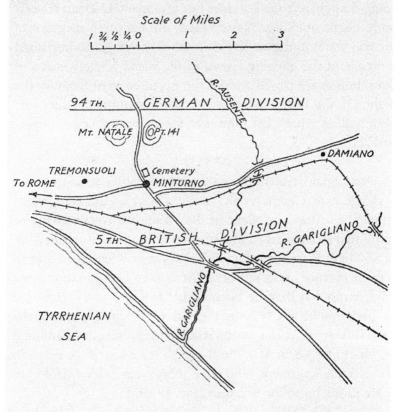

coastline, we arrived at Bizerte, a port perched on the tip of Tunisia, on the 11th and on the 12th of January we set out to make the crossing of open sea for Naples. This was the most perilous part of the voyage, but it passed without incident so far as we were concerned.

Our naval watchdogs reported only two 'contacts', meaning the potential presence of enemy submarines, which was heartening though, of course, it does not take many U-Boats to seriously blight one's day. Nevertheless, my enduring memory of the trip was nothing warlike, but rather the magnificent natural spectacle of the glowing crown of the island active volcano of Stromboli as we passed around the north coast of Sicily in the night. On the 14th of January we anchored outside Naples harbour and after breakfast moved to the shore and began disembarkation.

★★★★★★

Our initial destination was north of Naples at San Leucio, a village near Caserta at the western foot of the Campanian Appenines. After one night in the village we were ordered to move to a forward area and take over the position from the 40th Royal Tank Regiment. The 16th/5th Lancers had been sent to Italy in advance of the rest of 6th Armoured Division to join the 23rd Armoured Brigade because that brigade, which consisted of the Royal Scots Greys and the 40th RTR, and supporting the 78th Infantry Division was incrementally sending its constituent regiments to North Africa to train. We were to replace the 40th Royal Tank Regiment, who were at Sparanise which whilst not quite in the front line was very close behind it.

So, on the 15th of January we set out on a 30-mile drive *via* Caserta, Capua and Grazzanise, including a crossing of the River Volturno at Cancello to Sparanise. I was fascinated by the appearance of Cancello because I had never seen a town totally destroyed by war before. It would not be long sadly before this kind of sight was no longer a novelty.

During the afternoon we took over from our opposite numbers in 40th Royal Tank Regiment. Each squadron was allocated its space, but 'B' Squadron's originally designated area was badly flooded following heavy rain and we were compelled to share 'A' Squadron's area with them.

We were quartered in farm buildings which were dry, but which also accommodated a thriving colony of rats. We eventually became adjusted to their presence and troopers and rats coexisted in an atmosphere of uneasy tolerance. However, I was always in dread that one night, when lying on my bed, one of them would lose its footing whilst traversing the ceiling beams and come hurtling down to join me. The building which we occupied was used for storage of farm machinery and the floorboards were liberally coated in oil. The only light came in through the huge wooden doors and after dark we could only find our way about or read or write letters with the assistance of home-made lamps fashioned out of cigarette tins filled with petrol with a length of four-by-two-inch flannel inserted through a hole in the lid to act as a wick.

The rain was incessant; it came down steadily from a leaden sky and the tank standings were a sea of mud. It was extremely difficult to stay clean—everything was damp and most things covered in the mire.

As if predicted by these depressing conditions I then received some very sad personal news. In the contents of a letter from my Uncle Joe I learned that my grandmother had died. Only another week had elapsed before yet another letter arrived informing me that my grandfather had also passed away. The arrival of such news (I had been very close to my grandparents, having spent a great deal of time as a boy in their company) combined with the oppressive weather and uncertain future did little for my morale at this time.

★★★★★★

From briefings which we were given from time to time, we gathered that we were under command of the American 5th Army commanded by Lieutenant-General Mark W. Clark and would be working with 5th Infantry Division, consisting of the 13th, 15th, 17th Infantry Brigades and 201st (Guards) Motor

63

INFANTRY ON A TANK PASSING A BLAZING BREN CARRIER, DURING A
DIVERSION THROUGH A MINEFIELD

TANKS OF THE REGIMENT MOVING UP IN SUPPORT OF THE INFANTRY

Brigade. Our tanks were in need of an overhaul, having covered about 100 miles on their tracks since leaving Robertville in Algeria, and were also due to have some additional armour welded on, in the shape of special track plates.

We were told that our next operation would be the crossing of the River Garigliano by the 5th and 56th Infantry Divisions who would seize control of the pass leading into the Liri Valley. This would, it was predicted, open the way for our brigade who with the 16th/5th Lancers and 11th King's Royal Rifle Corps leading, would chase the Germans back up the peninsula and north of Rome.

However, the advance ground to a halt just north of Minturno village and it was decided that 16th/5th Lancers' involvement would consist of one squadron helping the infantry to hold Minturno and reinforce the rather insecure Garigliano bridgehead. This squadron would also provide support for an attack on Monte Natale and Point 141, north of Minturno. 'A' Squadron were the lucky lads detailed for this operation, and we in 'B' Squadron concealed our disappointment as best we could by taking the liberty bus into Caserta where we reluctantly enjoyed ourselves.

After a few days we moved forward to a harbour in a quarry on the outskirts of Minturno. I was at this time in the tank commanded by Captain Metcalfe, the second-in-command of the squadron, and was part of a totally inexperienced crew.

Our first exposure to enemy fire was totally confusing. We arrived in the dark and my first impression was of an incessant noise. There were explosions all around, guns, mortars, the chatter of machine guns, the night illuminated by the flashes of guns. I sat on the turret of the tank eating tinned chicken (not British Army standard issue, need I explain) and trying in vain to distinguish friendly from enemy fire.

Later we dug a wide but shallow pit alongside the tank into which we put our bedding rolls and over which we erected a cover consisting of the tank tarpaulin lashed to the tank at one end and pegged into the ground at the other. Unfortunately for

SHERMAN TANK IN THE GARIGLIANO REGION

Captain Metcalfe we had not made allowance for the additional depth needed for his camp bed, so he spent the next few nights sleeping at what was effectively ground level. The shelling was sporadic but quite heavy at times and I can remember him suggesting on several occasions that we might consider moving into the tank—a suggestion which was not taken up mainly because we could not believe we were in any danger. Our ignorance and inexperience must have sorely tried the patience of our crew commander, a veteran of the North African campaign, in which he was wounded.

War, if it does not end you before lessons are learned, is a good teacher and so it was not long before we were all as safety-conscious as the 'older hands' throughout the regiment!

★★★★★★

Two remarkable coincidences occurred here. I discovered a neighbour and ex-school friend of mine serving just up the road with the Loyal North Lancashire Regiment. This regiment had suffered the indignity of having their HQ raided by a German fighting patrol and had several prisoners taken. Fortunately, my friend was not among those spirited away.

Also, one morning after a particularly lively night of shelling and mortaring I saw a burial taking place over a hedge beyond our tank. After it was over I went to look at the grave and saw on the cross the name Signalman Albert Richardson, Royal Corps of Signals. Several weeks later my mother wrote to tell me that the son of our window cleaner, Albert, had been killed in Italy serving in the Royal Signals. It was, bizarrely, this young man's grave I had seen.

One day we had some welcome news. There were some showers, part of an army bath unit, in the area and we could all take turns to visit them. Off we went to enjoy the luxury of hot showers and clean, if not new clothing. Why does one always feel so much more vulnerable to shelling when naked? Our journey back was undertaken at a brisk walk, hoping to make it back to harbour before another salvo of shells caused us to fling ourselves in the mud, negating the benefits of the previous hour.

A Sherman passing through Lorenzo, 1944

★★★★★★

Eventually, what was known as the first Battle of Minturno was called off and we returned to Sparanise to wallow in the mud. Shortly after our return we were summoned to Squadron Office and told that Captain Metcalfe was appointing a new crew with the exception of Joe McWalter who would remain as driver, and therefore the rest of us would be placed in a pool of crewmen to be used as replacements. Shocked and hurt by this, I enquired as to the reason, but was told only that Captain Metcalfe felt that we did not get on together. This was even more baffling. We had a splendid relationship and had much of fun during our tour at Minturno. I have often suspected that Captain Metcalfe felt that we were too foolhardy and that our inexperience and lack of awareness of danger could have tragic consequences for all. He may have been right, but as I have re-marked earlier, we soon 'grew up' and our battlefield innocence did not survive that first experience.

It was around this time that we heard of the Anzio landings and before long 'B' Squadron was called forward for the second Battle of Minturno. This time I was surplus to requirements. Our happy band of replacements, sick and no-hopers remained behind at base while the rest of the squadron returned to our quarry. I spent most days chopping wood for fires and going out in lorries to railway embankments to collect stones to repair the roads.

Eventually the squadron returned, but sadly not unscathed. It appeared that a 105mm shell had landed on the road opposite 5th Troop who were preparing their dinner. Sergeant Vic Potts and Trooper Ray Creasey were badly wounded (Ray Creasey lost an arm) and others, including 'Paddy' Duffy (our only Irish-man and a protected species) were slightly injured.

It was now that we learned that our sojourn with 5th Divi-sion was over and we were to move to a new area. Before we left I was summoned by Squadron Sergeant Major Bert Am-brose and told that henceforth I was to be his wireless operator, replacing Jimmy Vincent who was being retired on age grounds.

It was policy at this time to impose a top age limit of 35 years on tank crews. I was certainly joining a venerable crew—driver Reg Jones, co-driver Keith Robinson and gunner Tom Barthorpe, who at 37 years old had a daughter who was not much younger than I was at the time. My new intimates were an experienced crew, used to dealing with Bert Ambrose who was a fierce disciplinarian, yet capable of a relaxed informality among his crew in action. As soon as we were out of action, however, his normal personality reasserted itself and we often felt that we were treated more harshly than the crews in the rest of the squadron in order to demonstrate to everyone that his own crew were shown no favours denied to others.

DOUGLAS MILES, 16TH/5TH
LANCERS—2NDNOVEMBER 1944

KEITH ROBINSON, 16TH/5TH
LANCERS

JOE MCWALTER, 16TH/5TH
LANCERS

TOPPER BROWN, 16TH/5TH
LANCERS

CHAPTER 8

Monte Cassino

The Italian campaign reached a point of stagnation.

The amphibious landings at Anzio, which began on the 22nd of January, 1944, had been a disappointment and gave rise to one of Winston Churchill's immortal quotations: *I had hoped we were hurling a wildcat onto the shore, but all we got was a stranded whale.*

Procrastination by the American general, John Lucas had led to a failure to advance when decisive action would have almost certainly brought success. The Germans quickly reinforced and held the invaders at bay. All hope of achieving of the original plan's objectives was now lost as the Allies were locked within a bridgehead with their backs against the sea and under continuous fire from the enemy. The idea had been to land in force behind 'The Winter Lines' and thus threaten the German rear. This would break the defensive barrier which opposed the main Allied thrust northwards and the two forces would then to link up to harry the retreating enemy. The problem was that no one inside the Anzio bridgehead was going anywhere soon and the main force was seemingly inextricably blocked at Cassino. For Churchill there were possibly chilling reminders of the Dardenelles landings which he had promoted and which all but ruined him during the First World War.

The monastery of Monte Cassino has gone down in the history of warfare as an icon of stubborn defence and tenacious assault. It overlooked the Liri valley, the town of Cassino and the River Rapido, and any movement by the Allies was observed and fired upon. There had already been two unsuccessful attacks on Cassino during January and February and the monastery itself had been bombed and largely destroyed without compromising its defensive capabilities. It has been written that the Italian Campaign with its fixed defensive positions, which required the hardest fighting to take, represented the kind of warfare that mostly closely resembled the trench war of the Western Front during the First World War. Nowhere was that a more accurate or more savage comparison than at Cassino.

★★★★★★

Now we were to be involved in a third battle to break the stalemate at Cassino. The plan was for the 2nd New Zealand and 4th Indian Divisions to attack the monastery from the town and the north. Then if the attack was successful, the infantry of 78th Division supported by the 16th/5th Lancers was to form a bridgehead over the River Rapido. The armour of the 16th/5th Lancers was to push on as far as possible.

We moved to the Mignano area and began training with the infantry. On the 15th of March the operation started. All day waves of bombers attacked the town and the monastery, reducing everything to dust and debris. During the nine days in which the battle raged, we moved up to a forward harbour, awaiting the call. Officers went out daily to reconnoitre the country over which we would have to advance, and various troops went forward from time to time to fire on enemy observation posts and other targets. Some troops of tanks went forward towards the Cassino railway station to create diversions and draw fire.

Apparently few our commanders thought that there was much merit in this plan. They were correct. Cracking Cassino would take much more blood and take much longer to achieve.

One day a Messerschmidt 109 fighter aircraft flew over our harbour very low and we all dived for our turret-mounted Browning .5 machine guns. In spite of the concentrated fire of the squadron's crack shots it got away unscathed. He never came back, though.

When not involved in the foregoing entertainments, we

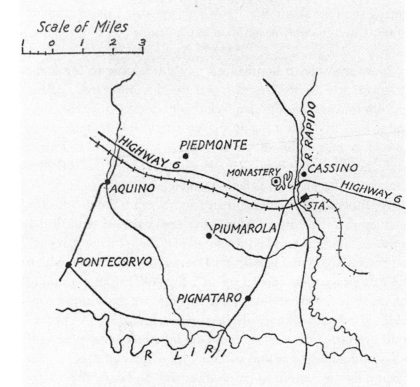

CASSINO AND THE RIVER LIRI, MAY 1944

Scale of Miles

tended to spend a great deal of time lying on our beds, reading, in the shelter of our bivouac which was attached to the tank.

★★★★★★

One early afternoon I was about to drift off to sleep when Captain Watson stuck his head in the bivouac and said that if I was not proposing to spend the rest of the war rotting in bed, he was taking a group on an ascent of the nearest mountain (the name of which escapes me), and I would be very welcome to join them. One does not refuse such invitations.

In truth, I was quite a keen walker. From being a small boy I had been taken on long walks by my Uncle Joe, my father, and my grandparents, who, though well into their seventies thought nothing of taking a six or seven mile walk after Sunday tea on a summer evening, and this was not unusual at that time. Hardly anyone had a car and to take a tram or bus for any distance under three miles was an indication of bone-idleness or having more money than sense. I had regularly walked eight miles a day to and from the Grammar School, and to the amazement and disgust of my fellow trainees had actually enjoyed our weekly route marches at Catterick.

This afternoon, however, added a new dimension to my pleasure. This was climbing, not advanced stuff with ropes, etc., but a sort of high-level scrambling. And when we got to the summit, the view was breath-taking, encompassing the whole of the Cassino area and the Liri valley, with the unpleasantness below visible only as puffs of smoke and flashes. We came down about two hours later and I was hooked on the pleasure of being in the high places for life. I indulged myself in them on post war holidays in Austria and Germany and the sheer joy of these experiences has never left me.

★★★★★★

By the end of March, the offensive was abandoned and we heard that the 6th Armoured Division was now in Italy, having stayed in North Africa for three months after our departure, and we were to rejoin the 26th Armoured Brigade and renew our association with the other two armoured regiments—the

CASTELFORTE 1944

17th/21st Lancers and the 2nd Lothians and Border Horse.

We accordingly set off to join the division in its concentration area at Piedimonte d'Alife. This was a wonderful change for us since mess tents were provided and we all slept in bivouac lines away from the tanks. I took the opportunity to scrounge some corrugated iron, wood and bricks and recreated a rather inferior but serviceable version of our Robertville residence.

Almost immediately we started training for the next assault on Cassino. We were to operate with the 4th British Division and several battalions came to stay with us and carry out combined exercises. Each battalion stayed with us for about four days and we entertained in turn the 2nd Royal Fusiliers, 1st/6th East Surrey Regiment and the 2nd/4th Hampshire Regiment. However, it came as no surprise to us when halfway through the final exercise with the Hampshires we were told that it was all off, and we would be working with the 78th Infantry Division when the battle for Cassino IV eventually kicked off.

The weather was superb and when not on exercises we spent a lot of time walking around the pleasant countryside. I spent several hours on these walks with 'Jock' Davidson, the gunner who was removed with me from Captain Metcalfe's crew. We were of a similar age and background and became good friends. Unfortunately, Jock had no chance to achieve the ambitions he confided in me on these outings because he was killed at Cassino not long afterwards.

A leave scheme was started whereby selected warriors were despatched to a rest camp at Amalfi. Those returning regaled us with wonderful tales of the delights awaiting us there. Unfortunately, everyone could not go to Amalfi in the time available, so a second rest camp was offered—the 8th Army one at Isernia. After the rest of my crew had been to Amalfi, one Saturday morning I was summoned to Squadron Office and told that I was going on leave to the rest camp at Isernia.

"Take small kit," said Squadron Sergeant Major Ambrose, "and don't forget your tin hat."

This seemed rather peculiar, but on arrival we soon found

out why the metallic headgear was *de rigeur*. The rest area was intended for troops newly out of the line and was considerably nearer to the enemy than our camp at Piedimonte d'Alife, in fact it came under occasional shell fire. We had left our safe camp, 30 miles behind the line, not to bask in the warm sun of Amalfi, but to lie with an ear cocked for the impending arrival of the next 105mm shell. We were there for only 48 hours and I was heartily glad to leave. The weather was dull and apart from a film show the only entertainment was a football match which was marred by an injury to one of the spectators who trod on an anti-personnel mine and lost his foot.

★★★★★★

It was quite apparent that with the improvement in the weather it would not be long before the push for Rome was renewed, and with a heavy heart I dismantled my little house and stowed my kit on the tank for a move to a forward concentration area which took place on the 12th of May. We spent a day harboured in this area awaiting orders to move and I spent most of the time sketching the surrounding hills and countryside in a notebook. I rather think I must have fancied myself as being in the tradition of the First World War poets who filled in the time waiting to go over the top by composing verse in their dugouts. At any rate, my work did not survive the war. I doubt if it survived the next day.

The plan was that the 17th/21st Lancers and the 2nd Lothians and Border Horse would act in support of the 4th British Infantry Division and the 16th/5th Lancers would support the 78th Infantry Division. The infantry kicked off on the night of the 11th/12th May and by the 14th the 8th Indian and 4th British Infantry Divisions had forced a bridgehead over the Rapido and a bridge had been constructed. On the night of the 13th/14th May the 17th/21st Lancers and 2nd Lothians and Border Horse crossed the river and at dawn on the 14th the 78th Infantry Division began crossing, and 16th/5th Lancers with 'B' and 'C' Squadrons up moved on to the left of the 17th/21st Lancers.

I remember that morning clearly. The weather was dull and

SHERMAN TANKS MOVING FORWARD IN WOODED COUNTRY IN THE LIRI
VALLEY, DURING THE CASSINO BATTLE—1944

misty and ahead of us we could see that the monastery itself was obscured by a haze of smoke which had been caused as a result the thousands of smoke shells poured into the area by our artillery in an attempt to conceal the troop movements in the valley from the ever vigilant enemy observers dug into the ruins of Monte Cassino monastery.

Nothing much was happening in our tank or outside of it for that matter. Keith Robinson was driving as a change from his usual duties as co-driver and to keep his hand in practice. The track leading to the river had been marked by parallel lines of white tape laid by the Sappers as they cleared the mines allegedly to indicate a safe route devoid of unpleasant explosive surprises. I looked across at George Thompson in the gunner's seat (I cannot now remember why he was acting as gunner unless Tom Barthorpe had been retired and George had stepped in for him temporarily) and saw him peering through his periscope. The wireless crackled with sundry routine messages from the regimental net regarding dispositions and priorities for us once we had crossed over the river.

With nothing to do, I took out a paperback which I had been reading over the past week—Richard Llewellyn's, *How Green Was My Valley.* I had read about half a page when there was the most almighty explosion and the tank shuddered and stopped. The force of the explosion blew the floor upwards and the chequer plating was displaced and buckled. Both the wireless sets were blown from their mountings and one hit me with some force on the back of the neck. The interior of the turret was filled with dust, and coughing and spluttering I scrambled after George to the turret hatch, ducking under the gun carriage with the extraordinary agility that comes when prompted by fear. As I stuck my head out of the hatch, George, who by this time was on the engine covers, was already speaking to Bert Ambrose and he shouted to me that we had just driven over a land mine A quick check of the crew revealed that thankfully everyone was all right and uninjured apart from a few minor bruises.

Bert, meanwhile, terrified of missing the forthcoming action and primarily mindful of his responsibilities as Squadron Sergeant Major, stopped the nearest passing tank, (which happened to be Bob Wake's), summarily evicted Bob from the turret and took possession of his Sherman. Bob came over to us as crew commander and, with nothing better to do and certainly with nowhere to go, we watched the squadron roll by into battle, giving us a succession of V-signs as they passed.

All through a very long day we listened to the progress of the battle on the wireless.

Gradually the field around us filled up with stricken vehicles as more mines were detonated. Our Sherman was in a terrible mess. The whole of the left-hand side suspension had been blown off; the track was laid out fore and aft in a straight line. It was obvious that any repairs to it, if they were possible at all, would take some time. Fortunately, we had sufficient rations aboard to get by for the immediate future and the weather was fine. During any excursions we made outside the vehicle we were, of course, careful to confine our movements to a path indicated by the tank tracks, as obviously—white tapes notwithstanding—the minefield was far from clear of mines.

I was finding it increasing difficult to keep abreast of the regiment's progress on the wireless as the action moved farther north, but on the following day I was able to pass on the news that both brigades had reached the first objective (code name, 'Grafton'), which was the Cassino-Pignataro road some 3000 yards beyond the River Rapido. There 'B' Squadron had called in a flight of P40 Warhawks which had flown in and strafed a farmhouse which was holding up the advance. The strike was successful and the strong-point was wiped out.

Some disturbing news came through on this day, however. Apparently our Commanding Officer, Lieutenant Colonel John Loveday was discussing plans with the commanding officers of the 6th Royal Inniskilling Fusiliers and the 1st London Irish Rifles when a 'stonk' of 150mm shells came down in the area. Several people were wounded, and in Lieutenant Colonel

Loveday's case so badly that he died on the way to the advanced dressing station. Major Gerald Gundry thereafter took command of the regiment.

The following day we were pleased to see the LAD (Light Aid Detachment) which came to begin work on the tank. The damage was so extensive, apparently, because the mine had been attached to a small bomb. It was going to be a long repair job, but we were glad of the company.

On the 16th the regiment had to deal with an enemy counter-attack which apparently was arranged to cover the withdrawal of the German 14th Parachute (Fallschirmjäger) Regiment from Cassino and the monastery that night. On the 17th, 'B' Squadron led the regiment as the 38th (Irish) Brigade advanced. The squadron was in support of the Royal Irish Fusiliers.

Also, the repairs to our tank were completed by late afternoon and after four days we were on the move again. We crossed the Rapido and trundled along in the fading light past the wreckage of battle. Bob Wake had his map with him but, of course, it had not been marked up during the last few days and at one point we discovered that we were the leading tank of 8th Army and charging down a sunken lane into the German lines. Fortunately, the infantry attracted our attention and we reversed to safety.

It was totally dark when we reached the squadron harbour to be given the sad news that only that day Major Gill, the squadron leader, had been killed and that two days previously, on the 15th, Corporal Harry Milner and 'Jock' Davidson had also been lost. A considerable number of men had also been seriously wounded. I had always regarded Major Gill as a father figure and it came as a distinct shock to me when, forty-five years later, I visited the Commonwealth War Cemetery at Cassino and found his grave, to discover that he was only 28 years of age. I suppose to a 20-year old, 28 years old seems quite ancient.

I threw down my bedding roll and dropped off to sleep almost immediately, only to be wakened by what appeared to be a fireworks display. All around us flares were dropping and soon we heard the sound of aeroplane engines followed by the screech and crump of bombs. They seemed to be uncomfortably close and we decided to take refuge in the tank. The troop concentrations in the bridgehead were intense and the Germans must have decided that it was worth having a pop at us before the attack gathered momentum. The following morning, we inspected the damage. Miraculously there were no casualties but there had certainly been a large number of near misses.

CHAPTER 9

Rome and Beyond

It was now the middle of May, 1944 and on the afternoon of the 18th, as Monte Cassino finally fell and the Polish flag was hoisted over its ruins, we moved to Aquino and spent the rest of the day just south of Aquino airfield under continuous shellfire. The Gustav Line had been broken.

On the 20th we moved to Piumarola where the 6th Armoured Division was concentrating. This was good news—we had done well with the 78th Division, but our real home was in the 6th Armoured Division and we felt that perhaps once more a part of it we might have the opportunity to take part in some significant armoured advances.

Two incidents come to mind now that occurred during our few days at Piumarola. We were on a rise, a small hill, I suppose, and as was customary when staying anywhere for more than a few hours we were advised to dig in. I was never an enthusiastic excavator and so in spite of the fact that the soil was soft and crumbly, I dug down only about two feet and slung my bedding roll into my personal trench. After a morning's maintenance on the tank we had a traditional tank man's lunch—tinned meat and vegetable stew followed by tinned fruit—and I then retired to my slit trench to read a copy of the *Sunday Express* newspaper, which had newly arrived from home.

I had scarcely begun to read when there arrived the most fierce and concentrated artillery 'stonk'. Several shells fell very close to my position and the shock from them caused the walls of my trench to collapse on top of me. I was quite literally buried, body, newspaper and all. Perhaps it was fortunate that I was too lazy to dig a really deep trench or I might have been in serious trouble since I would still have been buried though by considerably more of Italy than was the case. As it was, I ended up with a mouthful of finest Italian loam and was forced to spend an afternoon cleaning my clothes and bedding.

The following night I was lying in my trench (the same one, now slightly deeper) trying to sleep, when the potential for the experience was repeated. This time the artillery barrage was more concentrated and longer in duration. There was a real possibility of being blasted, buried or both together.

Feeling rather insecure, I considered the advisability of getting inside the tank. It would be safer to be ensconced behind armour, but to do this might be considered 'windy' by my comrades in arms. Cowering in my slit tench I stuck out this unpleasantness for about another ten minutes, but then decided to compromise my reputation, such as it was, and head for cover. Waiting for a lull in the explosive proceedings I sprinted to the tank, clambered up the side and flung open the turret hatch to scramble inside. To my surprise a cloud of tobacco smoke billowed upwards into my face and peering down through the gloom into the hull I could see the glow from the ends of three cigarettes.

"We wondered where you'd got to." said Keith Robinson, "We thought you were after a medal."

Evidently, my fellow crew members did not struggle with the issues of personal fortitude and peer evaluation to quite the same degree that I was prone to do up to this point.

On the subject of discretion being the better part of valour, I am reminded of a theory put forward after the war by an officer who fought at Cassino. His view was that we all start off with a personal stock of courage, rather like a credit balance in a bank account. Every time we go into action we spend a little of it until eventually, if we survive long enough, we run the risk of going into the red. This happened to men in the terrible

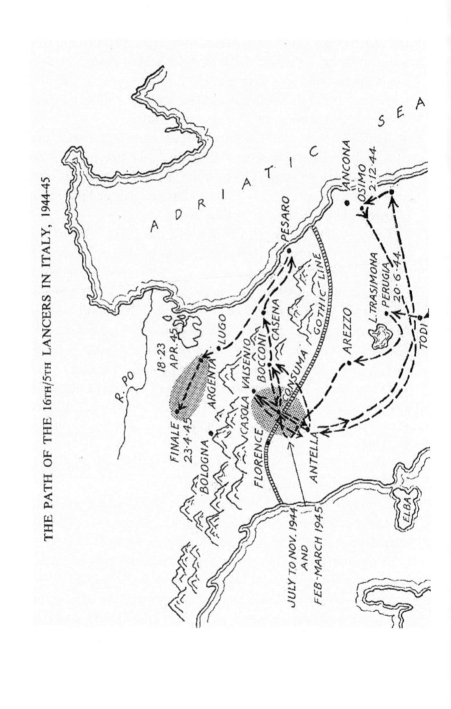

THE PATH OF THE 16TH/5TH LANCERS IN ITALY, 1944-45

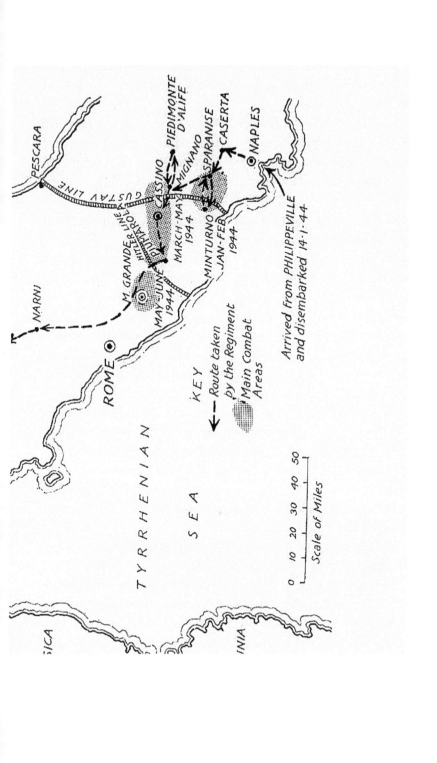

PESCARA

NARNI

ROME

PIEDIMONTE D'ALIFE

CASSINO

MIGNANO

SPARANISE

CASERTA

NAPLES

GUSTAV LINE

HITLER LINE TAROLA

M GRANDE LINE

MARCH-MAY 1944

MINTURNO JAN-FEB 1944

MAY-JUNE 1944

TYRRHENIAN

SEA

KEY

Route taken
by the Regiment

Main Combat
Areas

Arrived from PHILIPPEVILLE
and disembarked 14·1·44

SICA

INIA

0 10 20 30 40 50

Scale of Miles

conditions of the First World War and the army's response was to shoot them as cowards. Fortunately, a wiser attitude was present in the Second World War, perhaps because a lot of senior officers had been junior officers in The Great War and had experienced front line conditions.

Thankfully, I never emptied my 'account' of courage, although I have never considered that I did anything heroic. I sometimes think that maybe the bravest thing many of us did was simply not to run away.

★★★★★★

On the 25th of May the regiment moved off in the early morning through a thick mist and caught up with the Derbyshire Yeomanry who were in contact with the enemy at the River Melfa. On the way up to the firing line we passed a sight guaranteed to sink the spirits of any tank man—thirty-two Churchill tanks of the North Irish Horse all knocked out. We heard later that they had been caught when the mist lifted by a dug-in German Panther tank and several anti-tank guns. It was an impressive slaughter to behold and we proceeded in a more sombre mood.

The following day, the 26th, 'B' and 'C' Squadrons moved off in the lead at 06:00hrs carrying members of the 3rd Grenadier Guards on our tanks. We crossed the river into the bridgehead secured by 10th Rifle Brigade and made good progress for about three miles until we reached the village of Coldragone where we came under very heavy armour piercing fire from the foot of Monte Piccolo.

The advance was stopped; the infantry dug in and we pulled back a short way into harbour. We were now held up by two features; Monte Piccolo and the (naturally) bigger Monte Grande. On the 27th of May the 3rd Welsh Guards and the 2nd Lothians and Border Horse attacked Monte Piccolo, unsuccessfully. That evening the 3rd Grenadiers were sent to attack Monte Grande and the 2nd Coldstream Guards to Monte Piccolo. We were to support the Grenadiers and the 17th/21st Lancers were to support the Coldstreamers. We spent the day on the lower slopes of Monte Grande on a sub-feature called Point 206, a thickly wooded area held by troops of the German 1st Parachute Division. It fell to 'C' Squadron to take the brunt of the fighting, but we certainly did a considerable amount of shooting.

Just after our evening meal I was detailed to go forward and set up a listening post among the infantry positions and a few hundred yards ahead of our tanks. I approached it by crawling for what seemed an eternity along drainage ditches after which I spent the next six hours lying in a shallow depression awaiting the enemy.

The term 'Listening Post' presupposes that whoever might be manning it might actually achieve some 'listening'. As it transpired this was a fanciful notion because the entire night was filled with a riot of sound—the crash of shells, the wail of *nebelwerfers*, cries for stretcher bearers, the moans and screams of wounded infantry and the never-ceasing chatter of machine guns; the chug-chug of the Bren, the rattle of the *Spandau*, the hysterical screech of the *Schmeisser*, a sort of mad symphony conducted by the bringer of war, Mars himself.

Was I really supposed to hear the enemy creeping up on us? The Germans could have goose-stepped the regimental band of the Panzer Grenadiers past me bashing out '*Deutschland über Alles*' for all they were worth on that night and I would have been none the wiser. However, all good things come to an end and at first light, about 03:30hrs a runner arrived with the glad tidings that I could stop playing at foot soldiers and return to the squadron a grateful cavalryman.

As I made my way down the hill, I dragged a battered Woodbine cigarette from my pocket and lit up. Never had a cigarette tasted better. Many years afterwards when I was attempting to stop smoking and was weighing up the pros and cons of the matter, some devil's advocate of my sub-conscious would cause my mind to slip back to that day and reflect on the soothing effect that solitary Woodbine had on my nervous system. I arrived back in time for breakfast—two rashers of tinned bacon with two lumps of stale bread and a mug of hot, sweet tea.

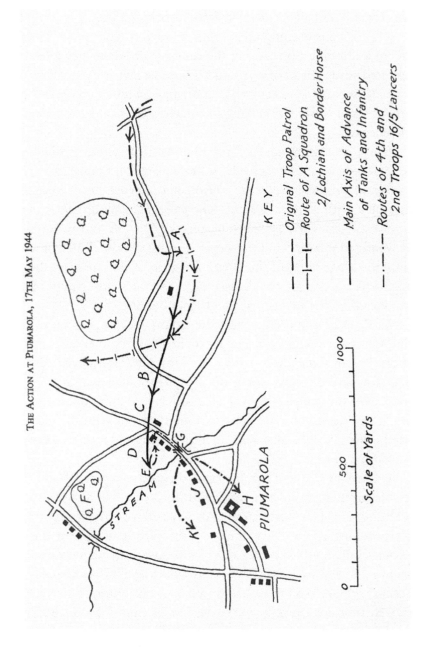

THE ACTION AT PIUMAROLA, 17TH MAY 1944

KEY

———— Original Troop Patrol

—|—|— Route of A Squadron
2/Lothian and Border Horse

———— Main Axis of Advance
of Tanks and Infantry

—·—·— Routes of 4th and
2nd Troops 16/5 Lancers

PIUMAROLA

STREAM

0   500   1000

Scale of Yards

Any hopes I had of making up for a night's lost sleep were shattered by the news that we were to pack up, load the tank and await instructions to move. The Germans had withdrawn from the immediate area and the Lothians and Border Horse had advanced at dawn and occupied Arce, about a mile ahead. Our move never materialised. Instead we pulled back a short distance and were placed on call for the 19th Indian Infantry Brigade. We spent a few days carrying out much needed maintenance and then on the 4th of June we resumed operations.

Our objective was Genazzano, about thirty miles onwards in our northerly advance. Considering our rate of progress so far, this seemed ambitious in the extreme. Our start point was Trivigliano and in order to reach it by first light we had to set off at midnight. It was decided that 'B' Squadron was to lead and at 05:00hrs we passed the start line and crashed ahead without opposition. After a time, we came across a huge crater and had to detour across country. On reaching Acuto we found it unoccupied and were embarrassed by an uproarious welcome from the townsfolk. On the other side of town another huge demolition held us up until Sergeant Jack Hillaby with 4th Troop found a solution and led us along a railway line for about two miles. By this time, we were beginning to enjoy ourselves and the speed of advance was exhilarating, as we rattled through Piglio and Serrone.

At one point the inhabitants of a village warned us of a minefield ahead and Sergeant Ord's Honey Troop located it and lifted the mines safely to allow us through. At this point we left the road to deploy and mop up some isolated German infantry and capture a few tanks. We had almost reached our objective by late afternoon and began to meet some resistance and heavy shelling. We were forbidden to advance further as we had outstripped the troops on our flanks and we were told to take up defensive positions for the night. It was here that we came across a gruesome sight. Looking through my periscope I saw a Bren gun carrier ablaze with the driver still in his seat, his uniform alight, and flames licking around his head. He sat upright, looking ahead,

SKETCH TO ILLUSTRATE THE ACTION AT PIUMAROLA.

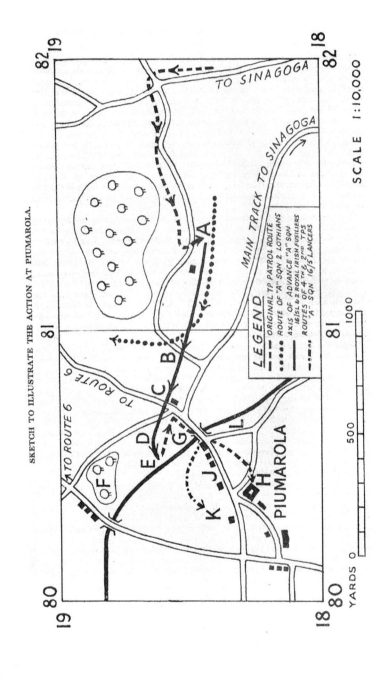

TO SINAGOGA

MAIN TRACK TO SINAGOGA

LEGEND
ORIGINAL TP PATROL ROUTE
ROUTE OF "A" SQN 2 LOTHIANS
AXIS OF ADVANCE "A" SQN
16/5 L & 2 ROYAL IRISH FUSILIERS
ROUTES OF 4TH & 2ND TPS
"A" SQN 16/5 LANCERS

TO ROUTE 6

TO ROUTE 6

PIUMAROLA

SCALE 1:10,000

YARDS 0   500   1000

for all the world as if he was on a routine drive.

★★★★★★

Incidentally, the 'Honey' tank was correctly called the Stuart M3. 'Honey' was a term of affection given to this agile light tank by its early crewmen that simply stuck and went into broader use. Reliable and easy to maintain, it was popular for reconnaissance duties because of its ability to 'shoot and scoot' since it had a faster turn of speed than most of its tracked rivals. Although the Honey's armour was only protection against small arms fire, its 37 mm M6 gun meant that it was never intended for extended armoured shooting matches.

★★★★★★

We had advanced 25 miles in the day and were accordingly rested the following day (the 5th of June), when the 2nd Lothians took the lead and made an advance of 35 miles, reaching the River Tiber four miles north of Rome.

'The Eternal City' had fallen to the American 5th Army on the 4th of June. General Mark Clark, commanding 5th Army, had political aspirations and was looking forward to post-war employment as senator, governor or even president! To be acclaimed as liberator of Rome would do no harm to these ambitions and we heard that he was so determined to achieve it he declared that any British or Commonwealth troops attempting to enter the city before the Americans would be fired on.

Our co-driver, 'Paddy' Hughes, on hearing this outrageous remark and bearing in mind the practical perils of being front-runner into places where the enemy might yet be lurking commented incisively that, "Anybody wanting to be first into anywhere deserves to be bloody well shot!"

The Lothians and Border Horse continued the advance on the following day, the 6th, and in order to catch up with them we had to endure a frightening night drive. The Lothians and 17th/21st Lancers met up with the enemy and had eliminated that portion of them by evening.

We had a quiet day in reserve, wondering how the news of the fall of Rome had been received back home.

"We shall be quite famous now," asserted Keith Robinson.

I had been on the wireless trawling the short-wave band and had managed to pick up the signal from the Forces programme in London. After listening for a minute a piece of momentous intelligence came into my ears through the headset. I turned to Keith and popped the bubble of his potential moment of fame.

"I don't think so, mate," I told him, "The Second Front's started."

★★★★★★

The invasion of continental Europe—D-Day—took place with the landings in Normandy on the 6th of June, 1944. This was the big news that everyone was waiting for and whether Mark W. Clark liked it or not few people were going to be talking about Rome any more. His moment of glory had lasted a little over a single day and nobody felt very sorry for him. A great achievement overshadows what was done to gain it, but a lesser one only leads to scrutiny of the degree of sacrifice that achievement demanded. That in turn leads to a critical examination of who was responsible. Clark focussed on liberating Rome, a city of no military importance, for its PR value to himself and in so doing ignored the order from his superior, Alexander, to primarily ensure that the German 10th Army did not slip away to fight another day at the Trasimene Line. Once more in strong defensive positions those same Germans caused more loss of life among the attacking troops than would otherwise have occurred and this unflattering consideration has become Clark's abiding legacy. Timing, as they say, is everything!

★★★★★★

The 7th dawned with the 16th/5th Lancers in the lead again, and it was soon apparent that the spell of largely unopposed 'swanning' was over. The enemy once again dug in its heels and 'C' Squadron ran into a force of enemy tanks. In the ensuing fracas we suffered a number of casualties including seven fatalities in two days. This squadron stayed in their daytime positions to support a night attack by the Welsh Guards while the other squadrons went into harbour.

Roadside halt of the 16th/5th Lancers, Appennines, 1944

The night attack was successful and next morning the Lothians went through to the lead position. They met very heavy resistance, but slowly moved forward with 'B' Squadron protecting their right flank. I found this a very unpleasant experience as we came under very heavy fire from anti-tank guns on Route 4, also a *nebelwerfer*, at very close range. This was eventually knocked out by concentrated fire.

At least the day's work ended early and we withdrew to harbour at 19:30hrs encouraged by the rumour that we were bound for a 48-hour rest break from the front.

At this time, we lost the Squadron Leader, Major Glen Illingworth, who was posted to 26th Armoured Brigade HQ as Brigade Major. Major Frank Watson took over and remained our squadron leader for the rest of the war, a stroke of luck for us, I think, as I considered him to be the most competent O.C we ever had. Captain Alec Simpson became second-in-command, an eccentric character who had the idiosyncratic habit of wearing a civilian hat and a predilection for marking up maps whilst perched upon his camp stool amid falling shells.

Whilst Captain Simpson may have appeared to be at one extremity of unconventional behaviour it was fact that conditions in the field were very relaxed on the subject of uniform and several of us, in best 8th Army traditions, sported very unmilitary items of clothing which erred on the side of comfort and practicality.

SERGEANT N. ORD WITH HIS HONEY TANK

CHAPTER 10

Into Tuscany

Our advance northwards now continued interspersed by a series of minor skirmishes. As we began our move towards Perugia, the Tiber valley narrowed and our tanks found it difficult, if not impossible, to leave the road. The Germans impeded our progress by demolishing the roadway and bridges. Land mines were frequent and the enemy regularly drenched us in shell and mortar fire. Shelling became particularly heavy in the afternoon period. One theory put forward to account for this phenomenon was that the Germans were heavily reliant on horse-drawn artillery and after a night withdrawal, their consequential and unavoidable slow rate of movement meant it was impossible to get their guns set up to greet us again before early afternoon.

We found this a most exhausting period of the campaign. We rarely arrived in harbour before 22:00hrs each day. Orders for the next day were given and we had our main (sometimes only) meal of the day. This was usually meat and vegetable stew washed down by tea, heated up on a petrol stove on the turret floor. Then the echelon would arrive with our supplies of food, petrol, water and ammunition. If the tank harbour was not easily accessible to the wheeled vehicles, we had to carry the supplies sometimes hundreds of yards over rough ground to the tanks. Then any necessary repairs and maintenance to the tanks and equipment had to be carried out and the wireless batteries checked, and if necessary charged. All these operations were carried out in the dark as the merest gleam of light would bring down a salvo of shells upon our position.

As wireless operator I was then involved in 'netting in' to the squadron frequency for the following day. These frequencies were changed each day to avoid detection by the enemy. I would send out a netting call and monitor the responses on my dials. Any stations not recording a suitably strong signal would be asked to re-net. Then and only then, could I consider my day's work to be done. Even so, I might be required to do an hour's wireless watch or sentry duty, so all in all I would be extremely lucky to get my head down to sleep before midnight, and frequently it was much later than that time. As the next day's entertainment normally began at first light (03:30hrs/04:00hrs), one had to drop off to sleep immediately to achieve even a minimum of three hours' rest.

After three or four days of this pressure, we were all literally in a zombie-like condition, and I can recall being left on wireless watch in the turret of our tank one day. It was late morning, the sun was high in the firmament and the temperature inside the turret was over 100° F. The rest of the crew were lying in the shade of the tank, enjoying the pastoral scene. The crackle of static in the headphones, the heat and total fatigue took their inevitable toll upon me and I nodded off to sleep. I was awakened by a standard issue army boot stamping on my shoulder through the turret hatch. On the other end of it I beheld the apoplectic visage of Squadron Sergeant Major Ambrose who had brought me a mug of tea. He spent the next minute outlining to me the various punishments he had in mind for my negligence which, according to him, could have resulted, in the worst of circumstances, in 'the annihilation of the entire squadron'.

In fact, we were at least five miles from the nearest German, were on a hardly urgent four hours' notice to move and in any event had the regiment been unable to make contact with me it would have found an alternative channel of communication very quickly. So I thought his reaction was a little over the top. But, of course, he was in the right. The army does not recognise extenuating circumstances and many poor souls during the last

R<small>EPAIRS BEING CARRIED OUT ON</small> R<small>OUTE</small> 67, 1944

unpleasantness we had, courtesy of these German gentlemen, paid for a misdemeanour of this kind with a guest appearance before the firing squad. I eventually solved the problem, should there ever be a repetition of such a blunder on my part, by passing the headset through the pistol port of the tank and sitting outside on the edge of the turret. Now, if I went to sleep I would quite literally fall off the tank. This was an admittedly drastic solution but, I reasoned, a reliably effective one since it is a very tired man who can fall several feet through the air and crash to the earth without stirring from his slumbers. Furthermore, this tactic provided an effective deterrent to incentivise me not to sleep on duty since to do so would bring the 'rude awakening' of idiom into harsh reality.

★★★★★★

We had a novel experience when crossing the Tiber. The bridge had been destroyed and, although we found a working ferry downstream, from our position it was not a feasible solution because it was not strong enough to carry a tank. We had to dismount from the Shermans and were ferried across to the opposite bank where we attempted to shovel away the earth to reduce the angle of incline of that bank to a degree which would allow the tanks to ford the river and successfully climb up the other side. We only managed to get two tanks across before the churning tracks made such a mess of the muddy bank that the third of our tanks to make the crossing stuck fast in the attempt.

The combined brain power of 'B' Squadron was put to the problem and came up with the solution to this impasse by using two tanks to pull each new arrival up the bank to safety. The whole squadron eventually made it across by the employment of this ingenious methodology, but we had been so delayed that we began to wonder if we would catch up with the war again. Some of us, it would only be fair to confess, were not particularly worried on that score and Keith Robinson commented that he was, in any case, 'convinced that the Germans would make sure we didn't miss anything'.

As we approached Perugia the enemy resistance intensified

TROOPER ALWAY AND CRAFTSMAN TAYLOR WASHING CLOTHES BESIDE
THEIR ARMOURED RECOVERY VEHICLE.

and we had to deal with increasing numbers of anti-tank guns and strong concentrations of their infantry in well-dug in positions. On the 20th June we entered Perugia as the Germans withdrew from the town and 'B' Squadron took part in a successful attack on San Marco accompanied by the Welsh Guards. We had been fighting continuously for five weeks and were now given the welcome news that we were to have a few days' rest.

We pulled back to Perugia, where the whole of the 26th Armoured Brigade was installed. We were billeted in a girls' school from which the girls, sadly, had long departed. The town was virtually undamaged but was under sporadic enemy shellfire which caused some casualties. There were two cinemas, each of which gave two shows a day and as the weather was kind we enjoyed our rest considerably.

Nothing lasts for ever however, and on the 30th June we set off in the lead, supporting 78th Division, but in true army fashion these orders were cancelled as we reached Lake Trasimeno. We were there allocated to work with the 10th Rifle Brigade in 61st Lorried Infantry Brigade.

The advance was resumed on the 4th of July and the order of march was quite impressive. It comprised in varying order, the 16th/5th Lancers, 10th Rifle Brigade, 12th Royal Horse Artillery, 8th Field Squadron Royal Engineers, and 111 Battery 72nd Anti-Tank Regiment.

There were about 150 vehicles in the column, which stretched for four miles, and I was probably not the only one grateful for the fact that the Luftwaffe had been largely driven from the skies. We must have made a very tempting target for enemy aircraft had there actually been any and a few months earlier when there were aircraft to spot us would have paid dearly for our temerity.

The advance got off to a good start and 'C' Squadron reached Castiglione.

Then the familiar pattern reappeared with roadway demolitions, heavy artillery shelling and attacks by small groups of enemy infantry and tanks. Our squadron was brought up to find

WRITING LETTERS & PREPARING FOOD, 16TH/5TH LANCERS

a way through between the road and railway, as the road was impassable until the obstructions had been removed and the craters filled in. We eventually found a way through and managed to advance slowly and tediously for about six miles. As it was by this time evening at around 21:00hrs we were told to halt and go into harbour.

We had lost two tanks which were ditched, but apart from that were largely unscathed. We had some unexpected light relief during the early evening when the eccentric Captain Simpson, complete with funny hat, organised a party of local inhabitants to fill in the road craters. He supervised this operation mounted upon a grey coloured pony which he rode up and down the road whilst trying to whip up some enthusiasm for the digging among his reluctant civilian fatigue party.

The following day, the 5th July, we were in reserve. We endured a day of very heavy shelling and as our movement was restricted it became quite unpleasant. It was never much fun just 'sitting there and taking it'.

We lost Lieutenant Colonel Gerald Gundry this day. His eardrums were ruptured by a shell which knocked out the Intelligence Officer's tank and he was evacuated to the Field Ambulance. Major Dennis Smyly took over the regiment. In the evening we harboured and suffered a particularly poignant tragedy.

We had been short of water and 'Gresh' Fincham, the water cart driver had brought his vehicle up and parked it in the centre of our position.

We on tank 555, 'State Express' (named for a popular cigarette brand at the time, incidentally) decided to use our latest acquisition—an aluminium kettle. Normally tea was brewed in a can, usually a 4lb jam or margarine container scrounged from the cookhouse, scalded out and fitted with a loop of wire to hang on the tank. These blackened but much prized objects were a feature of all British tanks, which in action looked like a travelling scrapyard, loaded as they were with bedding rolls, utensils and numerous bits and pieces 'liberated' from derelict villages to contribute to the comfort and well-being of the crew. One tank actually returned from an action with an upright piano which eventually found its way to the Sergeants' Mess and henceforth travelled in style with the echelon.

So our shining new kettle was a distinct civilising influence on our daily life and thus far we had only used it on a trial basis. It produced tea without the additional petrol flavouring and was voted a huge success by everyone who tasted its bounties.

The kettle was boiling and the tea about to be brewed when without any warning we were suddenly struck by a salvo of shells which, judging by the sound of their arrival, were 105mm calibre. The shells smashed into our tank harbour, crashing to earth right through the centre line. We all dived for the nearest cover, under the tank, within it, anywhere we could find which would to protect us from this lethal maelstrom of flying metal. After about a five minute pounding the shelling ceased and we crept out to survey the damage that had been caused. Our kettle was ruined having been thoroughly riddled by shrapnel. Much 'wailing and gnashing of teeth' from the crew ensued until such minor annoyances were put in their place by the news that 'Gresh' Fincham was dead, apparently killed by the same shell that destroyed our kettle.

He had taken cover in a ditch, but when the shelling stopped it was noticed he made no move to climb out of it. At first it seemed that he had no apparent injury, but it was found that a piece of shrapnel had entered the base of his skull. It seemed ironic that he should die in this way because he had already discharged his duty to deliver our water and so within about five minutes thereafter would have been on his way back to the echelon and comparative safety.

The *padre* was sent for, a burial party assembled, a grave dug, and within the hour 'Gresh' was buried in the ground and a cross erected over his grave. There really is nothing like war to graphically illustrate the frailty of the human condition and our personal insignificance in the greater scheme of things. An hour previously 'Gresh' had been sitting on the running-board of his

BRITISH SELF-PROPELLED GUNS NEGOTIATE BENDS ON THE DUSTY MOUNTAIN ROAD NEAR MONDAINO,
SEPT., 1944

tanker, enjoying a cigarette while we good naturedly took the 'mickey out him' as we front line soldiers always did with the men from the echelon, asking him how it felt to be actually up at the front for a change. Now he was just another map reference for the War Graves Commission to find later when he would be moved to a cemetery.

In civilian life when someone dies, the time between death to internment is usually about a week. There is no time to grieve in the sharp end of the army at war, which is perhaps a good thing for all concerned. I sometimes would worry that I was becoming callous, but then the knowledge that the next funeral could well be my own and that it would be dealt with in an identical manner tended to divert the attention away to more prosaic matters.

★★★★★★

The way I reacted to losses among my fellows preyed upon my mind throughout the war and for some years afterwards. A tank squadron does not always operate as a unit. When working with the infantry, often the individual troops (each consisting of 3 tanks) would spend the whole day isolated from each other, the only contact being by wireless to squadron HQ. At the end of the day's action, the squadron would come together in harbour for replenishment and repairs, and experiences would be related and news exchanged.

It was then that one would hear of casualties, and I was disturbed that sometimes after a particularly bad day, I would feel a certain light-heartedness, an elation almost, which was most inappropriate. I really felt there must be something wrong with me, but since we never discussed such matters I was unaware how others felt. Many years after the war I was reading an account of one infantry officer's battle experiences, in which he mentioned just such a feeling. His explanation was that the elation was not *schadenfreude*, but a relief that this time one had been spared.

As a herd of wildebeest, chased by a lion will settle down to peacefully graze quickly once the kill was actually made so subconsciously we are happy that we have survived yet again. I don't know if psychologists would agree, but this perspective certainly made me feel better about myself. Of course, wildebeest also know that a lion with a full stomach is not much of a threat, whereas war has an appetite for death which is apparently insatiable.

★★★★★★

I was involved in a very hairy incident at around this time. We were in support of the 10th Rifle Brigade on a hill when we came under the most intense shellfire. The infantry gave us a round cursing because the presence of tanks is never popular within defensive positions. They make a lot of dust when they move which alerts the enemy to their location and so attracts incoming shellfire. The 'Poor Bloody Infantry', of course, have to endure this very unpleasant treatment without the armoured protection enjoyed by the tank crews.

However, on this occasion we did not emerge unscathed. The tank was hit by two high-explosive shells; one hit the front transmission, fortunately doing no harm, but a second fell at the rear, liberally peppering our bedding rolls and reducing my best battledress to the appearance of a mosquito net (as I discovered later), but more seriously, puncturing the radiator. We began to lose water steadily if not rapidly, and our crew commander SSM Ambrose decided we should withdraw down the hill to find our fitters or LAD and effect a repair.

The problem was how to keep the tank moving whilst losing water. He looked around the turret and his eyes fell upon me with a look that made it clear that from his perspective the immediate problem had been solved. This, I felt intuitively, boded poorly for me.

"You're doing nothing—we don't need wireless," he declared. "Get out on to the back of the tank, open the engine louvres, take off the radiator cap and keep it topped up with water from the spare supply." We carried two four-gallon jerricans of water for washing, drinking and cooking lashed to the back rails.

"Great!" I retaliated, not best pleased as one might imagine, "Half the German guns in Italy are firing at us and I've got to stand five feet above ground level trying to pour water into a hole while you slide the tank down a bloody mountain! Why don't you just bury me here and have done with it?"

"Stop ticking and do as you're told" insisted Bert Ambrose, "you'll be all right, I guarantee it."

I have only the vaguest recollection of the journey down this hill except that it was a virtual nightmare comprised of a swaying tank under my feet, alarming hairpin bends, lethal enemy shells falling on all sides and the near impossibility of enduring it all whilst of directing the water from the jerricans into the small filler hole of the radiator. In the event, Bert's guarantee of my safety did not seem to count for much.

Eventually we made it to the bottom and safety and I slumped gratefully in the shade of the tank as we waited for an assessment of the damage. We speculated on the likely duration of our absence from action. Some said two days, some three; 'Paddy' thought a week. Oh joy! A bed under the stars away from flying ironmongery. Long hot days spent lazing in the sun, smoking, reading, writing letters. We had, alas, reckoned without the martial zeal of our crew commander. Bert fumed and fretted every moment he was away from his beloved squadron. I suppose we should not have been surprised at this reaction. After all, had he not already abandoned us once when we had been blown up by a land mine at Cassino?

Now he raged about, cursing, cajoling, wheedling, bullying until to our unbelieving horror, three hours after our arrival the fitter sergeant pronounced us fit and able to resume operations. In a cold black fury, we mounted and set off once again. Soon we were once more back at the top of the hill which I had so recently descended as though I was a living part a fairground shooting gallery target. As we moved back along the ridge the Germans delightedly welcomed our return with a few high explosive shells especially for us.

I felt as though I had a legitimate announcement to make.

"If they hit us there again, some other —— can stand on the back this time!"

CHAPTER 11

Towards the Gothic Line

We were now programmed to push on rapidly to Arezzo, but the attack was postponed for several days to allow the 2nd New Zealand Division on our right to catch up. This entailed spending more time in our present harbour, shelled from time to time, and very accurately, too. I was very pleased when we moved to another concentration area and short leaves were arranged at Lake Trasimeno. As usual 'B' Squadron were last to be sent, but eventually we put on our best KD (khaki drill) and embarked on lorries for a few days' rest.

Just before midday we arrived at this beauty spot and dropped our kit at a lakeside hotel. Here was sheer luxury! We had a quick lunch then quickly headed for the lake. By mid-afternoon I was lying half-submerged in the shallow water like a beached whale, soaking up the sunshine and anticipating the first rate dinner we had been promised. Suddenly we were summoned to get back to the hotel, told we had to dress immediately and be back on the lorries that had just delivered us within half an hour. Apparently the Germans had counter-attacked.

Back we went to the squadron in a state of utter frustration and misery, and as we de-bussed in our harbour area, an enormous artillery stonk crashed down as a macabre welcome. I threw myself into the nearest available depression in the ground for protection from the flying metal but was surprised by the revelation that my immediate concern was less for my safety than for the state of my best uniform which was by now filthy.

SHERMANS OF B SQUADRON 16TH/5TH LANCERS ENTERING AREZZO—16 JULY 1944

How was I going to get it washed and ironed now? I need not have worried in the event; I would not be using it for some time to come.

Once the excitement was over, I was told to set up a wireless watch for the rest of the day (and night) on some open ground nearby. I spent the next fourteen hours lying on my bed alongside a No. 19 set, complete with batteries, in an area devoid of any sort of cover. Fortunately, not a single shell fell anywhere near me during this entire period.

On the 14th of July the New Zealanders began their attack and the following day both 'A' and 'C' Squadrons were engaged. During the course of the next two days 'A' Squadron suffered eight fatal casualties. On the 16th 'B' Squadron pushed on and went through Arezzo to take up positions on the north and east of the town.

★★★★★★

The first 16th/5th Lancers tank into Arezzo was commanded by Reg Robinson who reminds me of this distinction practically every time we meet. This crew also featured in an often used photograph showing their tank passing some wrecked German hardware. Hollywood made them no offers as actors for action movies after the war. Wisely, they 'made do' with the talents of the likes of John Wayne and Audie Murphy instead.

★★★★★★

The war was now to change for the armoured regiments. From Cassino onwards we had been able to advance on our own without close infantry support, leaving the roads where necessary and often going across country to outflank the enemy. Now our axis of advance was through a narrow valley with steep hills on both sides and vines, trees and other obstacles making it difficult or even impossible at times to move off the road. The Germans were desperate to prevent us crossing the Tuscan Apennines before the winter weather set in, and to this end they employed every delaying tactic in use at that time—anti-tank and anti-personnel mines, booby traps, craters, felled trees and demolitions, every one under carefully planned and pre-ranged gun, mortar and small arms fire.

From this time onwards the two infantry brigades (1st Guards and 61st Lorried Infantry) took turns to lead with an armoured regiment in support. The advance was painfully slow but a welcome spin-off was an increased spell of maintenance and rest for the units not needed.

★★★★★★

On the 25th the 16th/5th sent a party of 150 to line the road for the visit of an 'important personage' who turned out to be His Majesty King George VI. I was not in this party but stayed in harbour with the rest of the squadron in an idyllic area with superb views across the valley of mountain villages and streams. We were between the towns of Terni and Narni and for reasons which have totally escaped me I was known within the squadron for the rest of the war as the Lord Mayor of Narni, a title still referred to some forty years later at a squadron reunion.

★★★★★★

For the next month we edged our way up the valley of the River Arno towards Florence, taking turns with the 17th/21st Lancers, Lothians and Border Horse and Derbyshire Yeomanry. The weather was hot and we ended each day covered in a fine white dust. The roads were dusty, the hedges and verges were dusty, our tanks were dusty and our clothes, hair and bodies were dusty, but we passed through orchards where peaches were abundant. The only enduring memory I have of this time was my 21st birthday. I spent it in a peach orchard in which the farmer had just perished after setting off a booby trap while attempting to pick peaches. A sad way to commemorate a milestone, but at least I was alive and well and in one piece even if there was nothing to drink. The regimental history of this time refers to 'a generous supply of cheap red wine.' The benefits of this apparent abundance of inexpensive vino certainly escaped us at this time, but in doing so no doubt prevented a lot of headaches.

On the 25th August the 16th/5th entered Pontassieve, where the Arno turns west to Florence, but much to our chagrin we were not directed at this fair city, which fell to the column on

A HONEY OF RECCE TROOP - 'B' SQUADRON 16TH/5TH LANCERS,
AREZZO 16 JULY, 1944

our left. From the Garigliano, where we started, to the Arno where we now were is 270 miles and we had covered it in 64 days.

The Allied plan was now to reach the Po valley before winter set in. Unfortunately, we were faced by the Apennine mountain range, some 40 miles wide, and a very determined German rearguard entrenched in their final defensive position in Italy—the Gothic Line. We were now part of XIII Corps, consisting of our 6th Armoured Division, the 1st British and 8th Indian Divisions, the 6th South African Armoured Division and the 1st Canadian Armoured Brigade. The objective was Bologna, with the primary object of preventing the Germans sending reinforcements to the Adriatic front, where the 2nd Polish and 1st Canadian Corps were attempting to seize Pesaro and then probe towards Cattolica and Rimini and capture Ferrara.

The 16th/5th Lancers were assigned to push up Route 70 which was, as it turned out, an optimistic description of the nature of our progress. 'Crawl' was a more appropriate description. We spent the next two months skirmishing along mountain roads and tracks which were often cratered and made impassable, so that an advance of a few hundred yards was deemed a success. Our route wound its way through the villages of Borselli and Consuma and climbed to 3000 feet in a short distance. The road was cratered, blocked by trees and liberally mined. Clearing these obstacles was an uncomfortable task carried out under accurate shelling, mortaring and small arms fire. There were heavy casualties among tank commanders, which were particularly upsetting collateral losses in what were really minor operations.

★★★★★★

About the middle of September, we were informed that the regiment would shortly be receiving new and improved tanks. An officer and three NCOs from the Royal Armoured Corps School in due course arrived among us accompanying two Sherman tanks. One of them featured a 76mm gun whilst the other tank sported a heftier 105mm gun.

★★★★★★

The development of the Sherman tank had undergone several experiments using 76mm guns but for various reasons these had proved problematic in practice so the standard form of the tank to this point remained, in most cases, armed with a 75mm gun. The problem in action, of course, was a combination of armour thickness and firepower when the tank came up against the invariably superior armour and firepower of its individual German counterparts during the latter part of the war. The 76mm gun was an undisputed improvement, though using its standard ammunition it would still only knock out a Panther tank, for example, at point blank range with a round positioned in a precise vulnerable spot on the enemy tank. These, as one might imagine, were singular circumstances that held little appeal to Allied tank crews given the likelihood and consequences of error.

Eventually, high velocity armour piercing ammunition was developed for the 76mm gun and this was equal to the task of destroying most (if not all) of its German armoured foes since it gave the Sherman real anti-tank capabilities. The down side of this good news was that there was very little of this ammunition in circulation for the 76mm gun and high velocity ammunition mostly went to those vehicles which were dedicated to anti-tank roles. The 105mm gunned Sherman firing high velocity shells was without doubt a very formidable tank of its time. The Sherman medium tank was manufactured in huge quantities (nearly 50,000 were made in its numerous variants) from 1942 onwards.

★★★★★★

One Sunday I found myself in the turret of the new 105mm-gunned Sherman taking part in a practice shoot. No full crew was necessary so there was just me and the gunner inside the tank. The squadron leader was standing on the back of the tank and about two dozen assorted officers and NCOs were loitering all around us, eager to watch the performance. The tank was drawn up in a sort of lay-by facing out over a valley into which we were going to discharge our shells at some predetermined targets.

The plan for the deployment of these tanks was intended to be that each squadron would have two 105mm tanks in its HQ Troop to act in support of infantry, firing mainly high-explosive shells; the remaining troops being fitted out with tanks carrying the 76mm gun.

The squadron leader gave the word to begin and 'on cue' I heaved the 33lb shell into the breech of the gun.

Major Watson gave the order, "Fire".

The gunner pressed the trigger. There was a dull click, then silence.

Following the laid down procedure which I had last used in training with dummy shells in Catterick, I gingerly opened the breech and peered inside at the base-plate of the shell which was, of course, still there. There was a tell-tale dent in the shell base-plate indicating that the firing pin had operated. This situation was now a highly dangerous one. The shell was likely to explode at any moment.

I slammed the breech shut and bawled at Major Watson "Cap struck!"

He and I both knew what had to come next. He organised a chain of not very willing helpers and then gave me the thumbs-up to proceed with the next step. Very carefully, heart thumping away, I opened the breech and very gently eased out the shell and passed it up through the hatch to Major Watson who passed it along to the next man in the chain and so on to the point where the last human link hurled it down the mountainside. Nothing happened. No explosion. Nothing.

Major Watson began the firing procedure once again

"Reload!", he ordered, then once he knew we were loaded, "Fire!"

'*Click*'.

My heart sank as I opened the breech.

"Cap struck," I reported according to the prescriptions of the manual, but what I was actually thinking was, "Oh, My God."

We repeated the firing procedure. To be precise and for the

A tank of B Squadron 16th/5th Lancers leaving Arezzo by Porta San Clemente, 16 July 1944.

record we repeated it nine times and every time we were re-warded by nothing more than a '*click*'. Each shell thereafter was carefully removed from the breech and manually passed along to its final destination down the mountainside, beginning its tenu-ous journey with of course, the hands of yours truly.

I had climbed into this tank a very young man. As I sat await-ing the order to load the tenth shell I felt 73 years old and every minute was adding another decade of wear and tear to my body and soul.

The squadron leader took pity on me and called off the ex-ercise. He was a little careworn too, I noticed. He had chewed his swagger stick down to half its original length. The offending gun was returned to Ordnance and we heard much later that the firing pin was about one thou short of making contact with the detonator. A manufacturing error had occurred, apparently. These little things are sent to try us.

★★★★★★

On the 26th of September we made another move forward. This coincided with a period of heavy rain and a decided drop in temperature. The next month was devoted to very minor skirmishing and frequently cancelled operations, often due to landslides and various other irritating occurrences.

By the end of the month the Gothic Line had been pierced, but at an enormous cost in wounded and loss of life. There was a severe shortage of troops due in part to casualties and also to the transfer earlier in the year of many experienced units to assist in the Normandy invasion.

The Gothic Line in common with the other defensive lines created by the Germans in the course of this campaign ran from coast to coast across the Italian mainland from the Ligurian Sea in the West to the Adriatic Sea in the East. It was perched across the summits of the Northern Appenines and was built by 15,000 slave labourers to include 2,000 well-fortified machine-gun nests, casements, bunkers, observation posts and artillery posi-tions. It would involve 1,200,000 men in the struggles to hold or take it and the bitter fighting dragged on inconclusively for over

Sergeant Ord and his Honey tank of the Reconnaissance Section attached to B Squadron 16th/5th Lancers, with delighted local partisans, Via Domenico, Arezzo 16 July 1944.

six months. Perhaps most importantly beyond The Gothic Line the Germans had prepared no other great defensive lines in Italy and at this point in the war they were poorly placed to deal with the advance of the Allies in open battle.

★★★★★★

We ended the month at Dicomano. My recollections of this period are of bedding down beside the tank in a quagmire. The rain was incessant and the slightest contact with the tarpaulin which we had rigged up beside the tank resulted in a stream of water descending on our beds. The general misery of our living conditions was compounded by a shortage of cigarettes. Most tank crews pooled their supplies; not only the issued items, but parcels from home. My mother regularly sent me a fruit cake which was much prized among the crew. Heaven knows what sacrifices she had to make in terms of wartime rationing food points in order to assemble the ingredients of this rare treat.

Cigarettes were shared, too—in times of shortage everyone contributed to the common pool. We were, therefore, dismayed when during a stock-check of this precious resource, 'Paddy' Hughes confessed that he had given away some of our coveted fags to an Italian farmer. Keith Robinson was incensed by the revelation of this unsanctioned act of generosity.

"You want locking up", Keith berated 'Paddy' who now appeared to be suitably contrite, "You'd give Hitler a bloody fag if he came round here asking for one!"

The mental image produced by this remark had the effect of somewhat restoring our good humour. What is particularly noteworthy is that Hitler didn't smoke so, irrespective of the many real dangers which were daily coming in Keith's direction from the *Fuhrer*, the scrounging of his cigarettes was not ever going to be one of them. A heavy smoker in his early years, Adolf had quit smoking and encouraged others to do so on the grounds that tobacco was a waste of money. Then, with the zeal of the converted, he instituted the first, largest and most influential national anti-smoking campaign the world had seen in modern times which was quite progressive of him when one

B Squadron HQ Troop 16th/5th Lancers, Gothic Line 1945.
From left standing: Squadron Sergeant Major Bert Ambrose, Doug Mills, Johnny Mutter, Sam Knowles. Kneeling: Joe McWalter, Al Offord, Wally Hopkins

thinks about it, especially considering he was a monster. Whilst on the subject of the predation of Keith's fags by the despots of the 20th century it is worth mentioning that his smokes would also have been safe from Mussolini because he quit in 1923. Stalin, on the other hand, was a chain smoker so potentially a menace notwithstanding that he was ostensibly on our side.

★★★★★★

I was astonished one afternoon to be told I had been granted a week's leave in Rome and was to prepare myself to leave within the hour. Presenting myself at the makeshift canvas structure which housed the Squadron Office I discovered that I was to have a companion on my visit to the 'Eternal City'. It was to be none other than 'Paddy' Duffy, a gloriously uncomplicated character with whom I had spent several hair-raising hours on sentry duty on two continents. I began to calculate the odds against staying out of the hands of the Military Police during the next seven days.

We left late at night in a three-ton truck, picking up several other lucky people from the other squadrons as we went and after driving through the night peered out from our Spartan transport at about 07:00hrs to see the amphitheatre of the Colosseum on our right. 'Paddy' was distinctly underwhelmed by this architectural icon of the splendour of the Roman Empire.

"What a dump." he pronounced, "Looks as though it's been bombed." So much for two thousand years of history.

We shortly arrived at our billets, in a barrack-like building about three miles from the city centre, from where we were taken daily into the centre in trucks.

I was determined to buy myself a watch—my previous one had succumbed to the North African sand—so I made my way to a jeweller's shop in a side street and found a suitable timepiece. The cost was 3200 *lire* (£8 more or less). This was four weeks' pay and almost cleaned me out; I had only brought 4000 *lire* with me on this jaunt. However, the watch proved to be a good buy, lasting for the next twenty years of use upon my wrist and being discarded at last only on grounds of its outdated and

'Paddy' Duffy and Sam Knowles in Rome

well-used appearance.

Given my acute shortage of funds, food was obviously going to be a problem. We were given breakfast at camp but the rest of our meals were required to be bought in Rome. The solution soon presented itself. 'Paddy' and I went into a Forces club on the Via XX Settembre to sample the char and wads and there I discovered a snooker room with six tables. Now, as part of a misspent youth, an ex-Grammar School friend, Jimmy McCabe and I used to frequent a billiard hall in Hyde. Jimmy had a small snooker table at home and was an excellent player, and I soon picked it up and became quite proficient. I was therefore able to challenge various unsuspecting soldiers to a game with a moderate side-stake and to the best of my recollection never lost a game at this time. The income from this activity was sufficient to purchase meals for the rest of our stay in Rome. Drinks, however, were out of the question, for me at least.

I discovered during a visit to the club that an English-speaking priest was conducting tours of the city each afternoon for a small fee, so I immediately signed up to go on one of them. We visited Mussolini's residence, the Palazzo Venezia, though '*Il Duce*' was understandably not at home to receive visitors. Next we visited the Spanish Steps, followed by a panoramic view of the seven hills of Rome from a wonderful vantage point. We then went through the crypt of a church which was stacked with the skulls and bones of long-dead monks, all arranged on shelves like goods for sale, and concluded our tour with a visit to St Peter's Basilica in the Vatican City which was fascinating.

This tour of Rome was a tremendous experience and I was very reluctant to leave the city at the end of the week. Even 'Paddy' enjoyed it although there were, he claimed, several gaps in his recent memory.

CHAPTER 12

Other duties: Roads and Red Crosses

We caught the truck back to the war and were not surprised to find that the regiment had moved. 'B' Squadron was stationed just south of Florence, in a small village called Antella. This was a pleasant location and the squadron was located in a rather impressive building, but we were not destined to enjoy it for long.

Almost immediately we were informed that we were to assist the Royal Engineers in road building. As I previously mentioned, the armies in Italy had been seriously depleted by the requirements of the Second Front, and the remaining formations were almost continuously in action. The engineers and infantry had taken heavy casualties and were sorely in need of reinforcements. As the armoured units were more or less immobilised owing to the weather and the terrain, it was decreed that they should help out with other sorely needed functions until spring made a resumption of the offensive possible for armour.

So ended any hopes we might have entertained of a comfortable winter cosseted with little work to inconvenience us. A group of us were taken in lorries to the unprepossessing village of Castel del Rio, from whence we sallied forth each day to break stones and fill in holes in the roads. Our billets were on the top floor of a rickety three-storey building. There was little to do in our off-duty hours except to sit on our beds and listen to the crash of shells outside, fervently praying that we would escape a direct hit, which would undoubtedly have consigned us to the role of hard-core in a new crater. Waste not-want not, as the saying goes.

★★★★★★

One thing I do remember about our time there is the quizzes we organised. Nowadays every public house and social club it seems has its quiz team, and the television schedules are awash with quiz shows, but during the war they were largely unknown. We in 'B' Squadron must have been veritable pioneers of the game, because I can remember taking part in troop quizzes in this place and previously in North Africa under the chairmanship of Lieutenant Henry Brooke.

★★★★★★

One afternoon I went out with a small, select party to reconnoitre a piece of road which it was thought might need our attention. We parked the truck in a village and while we awaited the result of a discussion between our officer and his sapper colleague several of us took a walk to the outskirts of the village. We turned around a bend to discover the road had disappeared. The Germans had demolished the bridge over a ravine, and there was a gap of about fifty yards of clear air between our stretch of road and its continuation on the other side which thereafter curved round the mountainside and away into enemy territory.

As we stood surveying the scene, I uncannily felt the hair on the nape of my neck stand up. It was a very strange sensation. Although there was no one in sight, I had a feeling that we were being watched, and an urgent desire came upon me that we should get away from this place as far and as fast as it was possible to do so. We walked back through the village to be told that nothing would be done until the following day and we were to leave immediately. Needless to relate this news could not have been more welcome. We promptly departed and for me it was something of a relief.

We were told the following day that only two minutes after we had left the most enormous 'stonk' came down, obliterating the houses, road and remains of the bridge approach. My premonition of imminent impending disaster, if that's what it was, was amply vindicated.

After a week we returned to Antella and began to take delivery of our new tanks. I also managed a day's leave in Florence which I found an attractive city, steeped in history and with a plethora of palaces and art galleries. The famous Ponte Vecchio had been spared the general destruction of bridges and the city as a whole had escaped too much damage.

★★★★★★

One day we were told that we would be required to spend some time up in the front line with the infantry as stretcher bearers for the wounded. We were to take greatcoats, small pack and spare pair of boots tied together by the laces and hung around our necks.

We travelled for what seemed like most of one afternoon and were dropped off in pitch darkness in a shell-pocked and cratered village where we were instructed to fall in and proceed under the direction of guides. Here we were told to dump our packs and boots in a farmyard. We were to recover them after the operation, which in typical army fashion, made it pointless to have brought them along with us in the first place. We felt we would be lucky to see them again.

Now we were afoot and set off beyond a battery of American 155mm guns, over a stream and upwards into the foothills. As we progressed, various groups were detached and led off along tracks to their destinations.

The track became steeper and harder to climb. The incessant rains had turned the ground into a quagmire and we were literally wading up to our knees through liquid mud. Several people began to complain that they could go no further and were consequently dropped off at the next forward aid post. I was tenacious (or foolish) enough to plod on uncomplainingly and paid for it one way or the other before long. After about three miles of almost vertical incline covered in mud there was just four of us remaining in the group, under the command of Corporal Les Crafter. Finally, we arrived at the last aid post, which was position just behind the most forward infantry positions.

Our future home was a cave in the hillside where, in the last stages of exhaustion, we gloomily surveyed the interior. Some attempt had been made by previous residents to provide seating for its occupants by cutting into the rock walls, but that was all the comfort on offer so it was apparent that any sleeping we might attempt would have to be done upright in a sitting position.

First aid supplies were contained in metal boxes stacked against the rear of the cave and the whole unsavoury mess of this place was presided over by a weary Royal Army Medical Corps sergeant. Fortunately, in view of our temporarily depleted physical conditions, our first night as troglodytes was uneventful.

The military theory behind this system of aid posts was that since the positions were inaccessible by jeep, any casualties had to be manhandled down the mountain *via* a series of stretcher stations, each group of bearers handing over their burden to the next group and then making their way back to their base. In the dark and under enemy fire it was a most unpleasant experience and the unfortunate casualty was lucky if he reached the Casualty Clearing station in the village within three or four hours and without being tipped off the stretcher several times *en route*. Not surprisingly, the more seriously wounded men did not survive such a journey.

The Germans treated us with typical Teutonic bureaucracy. We had a Red Cross flag and when we went out bearing it aloft they would not fire on us. But step out just a few feet without it and you would get a salvo all to yourself, something I discovered early on the second morning when I made the mistake of going out some distance from the cave to relieve myself without a flag to announce my harmless intentions. The madness of it all was apparent when you consider that we were under constant observation from the enemy who were close enough to recognise us through their binoculars as individuals. They knew what we were doing there and common sense should have dictated that they withhold fire whether we had the Red Cross flag or not. But there it was, and the transgression of this German precise code of requirements on the subject was to have tragic consequences on the third day we were there.

About mid-morning we were visited by a young infantry-man from the battalion in front of us. He had come up from base and was accoutred with small pack, rifle and entrenching tool. In common with all our visitors he had great difficulty in speaking at first, the climb having driven the last vestige of air from his lungs. We gave him a cup of tea and he told us that he had been sent to dig a slit trench for his commanding officer. The Royal Army Medical Corps sergeant was uneasy about the fact that he had entered our cave bearing arms since the Germans being particularly strict about this contravention of the principles of Red Cross facilities.

Sure enough, within a few minutes there was a great whoosh as a salvo of shells straddled our cave. We crouched along the walls to obtain what little cover was available, but one shell fell right in the entrance. I felt a blast, a twitch of my beret and a blow on my arm. I looked up to see half a loaf, covered in blood, lying in front of me. There was a strange gurgling, bub-bling sound filling the air. I looked around to discover what was causing it. The RAMC sergeant had already moved to the back of the cave. Our visitor was lying half propped up against the wall with blood pumping from his throat. He had been hit by a piece of shrapnel and the bubbling noises were his attempts to breathe. To my untrained eye he looked as though he was 'a goner', but the RAMC sergeant took a field dressing and with reassuring words began bandaging him. It seemed a hopeless task, however, because soon the poor lad's body, his uniform and all of us were soaked in his blood.

"Let's get him back," said the sergeant.

I laid my greatcoat over him; a futile gesture, but I felt better for having done something, and off we went through the mud.

As we approached the halfway mark between our post and the next, I went on ahead to warn the next station so that they could meet us and take over with a minimum of delay. It was my first visit to this post and I was not familiar with the approved route, so after about five minutes I found myself approaching the house (their accommodation was superior to ours) across a field dotted with corpses of cattle, horses, and mules and littered with abandoned military equipment. My unease was not diminished by the sight of an enemy notice lying in a shell hole alarmingly declaring, "*Achtung! Minen!*". I had wandered into a minefield and I was so far into it at this point that it would be just as dangerous to retrace my steps as to press on.

The rest of my journey took about three more minutes, as well as I can recall, but it was without doubt, the longest three minutes of my life. With every step I took I expected to hear the ping of a land mine detonator but I dared not stop to examine the ground before I trod upon it because the stretcher-bearers carrying our casualty were already within a few hundred yards of where the next team would need to take over from them. So I pressed on, hoping for the best, and coming through the danger at last alerted the post of the urgency of what was coming their way as instructed.

I slumped into the nearest chair. My heart was racing and in spite of the outside temperature I was sweating profusely and felt totally physically and mentally drained. Bill Gidman, in charge of the post, organised a cup of tea for me while his stretcher-bearers went out to take over from the incoming team. Shortly afterwards Lieutenant Graeme Thorburn arrived. He was in charge of the 16th/5th Lancers detachment of stretcher-bearers. After we had chatted for a couple of minutes he suggested we got off back to the cave. I really was not ready to leave quite yet so I asked if I could have a couple of minutes more for recuperation I left. He looked at me very intently.

"I think perhaps you had better not go back there just yet," he said, "I'll send someone else up and you can come back with me for a rest."

After a while we walked back down the mountain. It looked totally different in the light of day. Down below us we could see the positions of our left flank forward troops, the Royal West Kent Regiment, small smudges of khaki in holes in the ground with the puffs of smoke from shell bursts scattered among them.

During the whole journey back to base Lieutenant Thorburn kept up a steady conversation. There was plenty to talk about because we were old adversaries on the subject of politics, and as a New Zealander he took a very liberal view of military protocol. On active service, in our squadron at least, the atmosphere between officers, NCOs and men was quite relaxed. We ORs were allowed a great deal of latitude in our daily conversation but strictly on the understanding that any familiarity did not confer the right to query or dispute orders.

No reference was made to the events at the cave though I was profoundly disturbed by the occurrence. What had happened to me? Was I 'bomb-happy'? Obviously Mr Thorburn thought I was not quite myself, otherwise he would not have suggested I came back with him for respite. Certainly, after the shelling, I was calm enough. I had assisted in the treatment of the casualty and had the presence of mind to put my coat over him, I had seized the Red Cross flag to prepare our exit and ensure we were not fired on. It is very difficult to analyse events when it is your own perception of them that has been impaired.

I have often thought about this incident since those days and have come to the conclusion that the episode in the minefield possibly pushed my nerves too far. At any rate whatever damage I sustained was not long lasting. I spent the next few days working around the base and then returned to the forward area and into the farmyard where we had left our packs and boots. As I feared, they had disappeared. Stored in my pack were my personal belongings, writing paper, letters, addresses, housewife repair kit and shaving tackle etc. All gone. All I had left was the clothing and equipment I was wearing. Even my greatcoat, a necessity in the perishing winter cold, had gone, though at least that had been in a good cause to cover the wounded infantryman.

I noticed an odd lump in my beret and on closer examination found a small piece of shrapnel still lodging there. That potentially fatal tiny fragment of metal was obviously the cause of the twitch I had felt when the shell struck. Had its trajectory determined it would arrive at my head an inch lower I would have been the subject of a War Office telegram of condolence to my parents. To make matters worse, I made enquiries among the medical team and discovered that the young infantry lad we had carried down the hillside had, despite everybody's best efforts, tragically died as a result of his injury.

Eventually we returned to Antella and a Court of Inquiry into the loss of our equipment. I testified before a panel of officers and was indignant when we received a reprimand for being careless with HM Government's property. At any rate no punishment was awarded, and we were issued with replacement kit.

CHAPTER 13

Lancers as Infantrymen

We had now received our new tanks and were beginning to familiarise ourselves with them. Our tank was a 105mm-gunned Sherman with a huge Pratt & Whitney radial engine (no more death-defying rides on the back of the tank topping-up damaged radiators). These were wonderful engines which had, of course, been originally developed for use in aircraft. They were more reliable than conventional inline vehicle engines of that time and offered a greater power-to-weight ratio. In tanks they had one down side which was that they had to be mounted vertically which, since they had a larger diameter than inline engines, increased the height of the tanks silhouette. No tank soldier, understandably, wants his tank to be more conspicuous. These new Shermans no longer used diesel fuel, but ran on petrol instead

"That should make it burn even better," pronounced Keith Robinson by way of dubious gallows humour.

Out of the blue, at the end of November, we were told that the whole of the 26th Armoured Brigade was to move to the east coast of Italy, our destination being a little hill town called Osimo, just south of Ancona. Before we left Antella we held a squadron dance which was mainly memorable for the vast amounts of vermouth consumed by the tank crews. Marsala, too, proved popular and Reg Robinson's efforts in that direction were generally held by some theorists to be responsible for the shortage of that beverage until approximately 1952.

We left Antella on the 1st of December and arrived in Osimo on the evening of the next day. The tanks were carried to their destination by transporter. We were billeted in a house on a hill with our tanks parked some 400 yards away at the foot of the hill, alongside the road. We slept on cold marble floors and I can distinctly remember shaving in the great outdoors in cold water, my mirror propped up on the windowsill, in a snowstorm.

Just as we were beginning to anticipate Christmas, we were shocked, on the 17th, to learn we were to be sent to Riccione on the Adriatic coast to take over some very old Sherman tanks, preparatory to their embarkation to Greece. We lived in beach villas and our tanks were parked on the beach. They were battered and filthy, and our particular example had bloodstains and pieces of unidentified substances hanging from the turret walls. Obviously something extremely unpleasant had happened to the previous owners, and although we were not overly superstitious, we did not fancy going to war in such ill-fated machinery. However, we worked hard and long and after a few days had made the tanks inhabitable—how they would perform mechanically was another matter. We were unenthusiastic to say the least, and our mood was not improved by the news that we were to embark on the morning of Christmas Eve. Then, wonder of wonders, at 10:00hrs on the 23rd of December we were told the whole operation had been called off which as Christmas gifts go was a particularly welcome one.

★★★★★★

Back we went to Osimo and a reunion with our new tanks. By 18:00hrs on Christmas Eve we were ready for the festivities. And what festivities they were. On Christmas Day we had a Carol Service, after which Reg, Keith, Doug Miles and I paid a lengthy visit to our favourite wine bar where we drank our way along the top shelf and partook liberally of the bowls of almonds our host had provided for us. Later we had an excellent Christmas dinner accompanied by plentiful quantities of *vino* and beer, served to us according to regimental custom by drunken sergeants.

A Sherman in the Apennines, winter 1944.

The weather had now became very cold and snow fell very heavily. We had a regimental dance where I sampled Italian gin and brandy with disastrous results for my head. Osimo was a splendid little town, even if we did get sniped at from time to time when visiting the tank park. No one was ever caught rifle in hand and we never found any explanation as to why this annoyance happened. Perhaps some disgruntled local fascist felt the need to make his sentiments felt. The rest of the population, however, could not have been more friendly towards us and I could have quite happily ended my war in Osimo.

It was not to be, of course, but the next phase of the campaign was to give a palpable shock to 'mounted' troops. On the 14th January 1945, we were ordered back to Antella to prepare to act as infantry in the mountains. We handed over our new tanks for the third time, but we were promised that we would get them back later.

On arrival at Antella, we were installed in our old quarters and were quickly issued with special clothing. There were string vests (a novelty indeed), windproof jackets, white suits for patrolling in the snow, white duffle coats and many other strange and desirable articles.

Training as infantrymen also began. As it was only a matter of two and a half years since I had undergone basic training in infantry tactics and weapons, I was immediately at home. A lot of my colleagues, however, had never tasted the delights of foot-slogging and were clearly unhappy. I can still recall the occasion of a route march, when rigged up in full kit, we were ordered to double march. The order was received with a stunned incredulity, and had to be repeated twice before it registered. Most of these lads only broke into a trot for pay parades and when heading for the cookhouse. We also practised night patrols and one night I got lost and came back with another patrol, only finding out the error when we emerged into the light of the billets. Joe McWalter declared he was not impressed.

"If that had been a real operation, you could have gone back with a Jerry patrol, and you've got the only pack of playing cards," he said. It is nice to know that people care.

The general opinion was that the whole exercise had hardly been worth the trouble of blacking-up our faces.

At last we were given our assignment. We were to relieve the 10th Rifle Brigade in the mountains at a place called Casola Valsenio, and at the end of the month we moved forward to the village in preparation for our take-over.

Front line areas are unmistakeable. This is the world of the infantry and there is no mistaking when one has crossed the boundary to enter into it. Traffic moves that bit faster. Drivers hurtle past, their faces fixed with set expressions, as if to say "Let me through. This is not a good place to be." Hedges and ditches are festooned with telephone wires. Unit signs and warning signs proliferate.

"Watch your Dust!" "Under observation" "Dust brings shells".

Men walk with sunken, lifeless eyes dragging their weary bodies back from the line, to grab a few days' sleep and a bath, before they go back up into the firing line again. And above all there is the smell. Over everything there hung a miasma of dead cattle, dead horses, dead mules and dead men-all smell alike. On the front line the smell is the greatest sign of them all. It announces, 'Here is Death. You have arrived'.

The positions could only be reached on foot. The track up to the ridge on which they were located was so difficult as a consequence of thick snow that even jeeps with chains could not get through. This meant that all supplies and ammunition had to be taken up by pack mule, a journey which took about an hour and a half each way. We were accordingly instructed in the art of loading and unloading supplies on mules so that we could assist the Indian Army muleteers when they visited us each night in the front line. The instruction took place in Casola village square. Just off the square was a ramp down to the river, with a high wall on one side, to which the mules were tethered. This left about a yard of free access to get past the mules and it was a highly dangerous manoeuvre, as the mules took a sadistic delight in lashing out just as someone was passing. The Indians thought their

TROOPER L WALKER SCANS AN ENEMY HELD HILL FROM HIS STRONG POINT, 1945

mules were wonderful, but try as we might we could not learn to love them. We were, however, to be grateful for their efforts in braving the elements and the shelling to bring us our supplies and most important of all, our mail every night.

The sector of front occupied by the Regiment only required one squadron in the front line. This made the dispositions as follows:—

One squadron in front line.
One squadron in Casola.
One squadron in reserve in Antella.

As ever, 'B' Squadron was awarded the questionable honour of being first in the lines, and on the night of 2nd/3rd February we stepped out from Casola and wound our way, slipping and sliding and cursing profusely to yet another new adventure in the mountains. Our positions consisted of four small houses spaced out along the ridge. Three of these dwellings took in a troop each and the fourth, on the extreme left, was occupied by Squadron HQ and a gunner observation post.

As a wireless operator, I now became a signaller and would be responsible along with my colleagues for going out to mend any breaks in the communication lines which might be caused by enemy shelling. This was not a job coveted by anyone since it entailed crawling whilst running the line through your fingers until you came to the break, then fumbling in the dark with pliers and insulating tape to effect a repair, in the knowledge that the precise location in which you crouched had been, by virtue of the necessity for your being at it, recently the recipient of a shelling. It was not unusual to have to go out several times during the night and our numbed fingers were kept permanently crossed during these sorties.

As we took over I had the chance of a few words with my Rifle Brigade counterpart. He told me it was reasonably quiet and not a bad place to be at all. They were going, he said, to prepare to put in an attack on Tossignano. We wished each other luck and he sloped off into the night.

The following morning dawned bright, cold and sunny and we were able to take stock of our surroundings. Our ridge was faced by another ridge about 500 yards away. This ridge, which contained the German forward positions had a cliff-like face and was considerably higher than our ridge. Our task was to defend our ridge against attack and dominate no man's land by patrolling. Every night we sent out patrols. We erected a system of trip wires and flares in front of our positions, as the Germans also sent out patrols and were fond, according to the men of The Rifle Brigade, of firing off *panzerfausts* at our houses. This early warning system was not a particular success at first. We had a couple of sleepless nights standing-to as a result of flares going off, until we realised that they were being set off by rabbits and livestock from the deserted farms wandering around in no man's land during the night. We set the wires higher off the ground and the problem was solved.

Shelling and mortaring was fairly frequent, but our houses were sturdy and for the first few days we suffered no serious damage. I found myself a bed space on the floor of a room the outer wall of which faced the enemy. This made it vulnerable to shelling so no one else wanted it and I felt that the luxury of a private room was worth what I believed to be only a slight additional risk.

★★★★★★

One morning I got up and went into the kitchen to see if anyone had made some tea. I glanced towards the fireplace where a roaring fire was driving away the early morning chill in the air and, upon realising what else occupied the room, felt my eyes stand out like the proverbial chapel hat-pegs. There, sitting by the fire, quietly drinking a mug of tea, was a private soldier of the German Wehrmacht.

What was even more astonishing was that this one had the damned cheek to look just like me! There he sat with his red hair and his fair complexion. We even had the same physical build. Only the uniform he was wearing was different to mine. I looked at him dumbly.

BREN GUNNER 1945

"*Guten Morgen*" said my *doppelganger* politely as he noticed me. "Morning" I replied with equal civility.

It was a ridiculous situation on the face of it (if the pun can be excused), but how is one supposed to behave in such circumstances? I was quickly put in the picture. Apparently this soldier had been a member of an enemy patrol which had come under our fire about 200 yards in front of our position. His friend had been badly wounded in the skirmish and in order to get medical help for him this young man had crawled to our forward posts and had given himself up. He was to be taken down to the village shortly, to be interrogated and then sent to a prisoner of war camp.

He told me he was 19 years old and before he was conscripted into the army had been a student at Leipzig University. Furthermore, he told me that hated the war and had no great talent for soldiering. There is a certain affinity between all front-line soldiers, whichever side they are fighting for. They have more in common with each other than with their own 'base-wallahs'. They share the same discomforts and dangers, the same hopes and fears and I felt no animosity towards our guest and hoped, as he left on his way to captivity that he would be treated as well from this point onwards as he had been treated by us.

On the sixth day on the line tragedy struck. One of our houses had been damaged by shellfire and it was decided to move the troop that had occupied it into an unoccupied house further along the ridge. Sergeant Shuttleworth entered this house to inspect the facilities it might offer, but unknown to us it had been booby-trapped by the enemy. Suddenly we heard an explosion from this house followed by cries. Sergeant Shuttleworth was badly hurt by this trap and as he was taken past us, strapped to a mule on his way to the CCS his appearance prompted us to fear the worse. Our concerns were unfortunately justified, for later in the day we were saddened to learn that this very popular NCO had died.

Two days later, we had some more welcome news. We were to be relieved by 'C' Squadron in two days hence.

★★★★★★

That night, when the mule train arrived we unloaded it and decided, as a gesture to good housekeeping, to send back a quantity of used and unwanted gear in preparation for our relief. We loaded the stuff into ammunition boxes and carried it outside to where the mules waited.

It was a golden rule for everyone to be as quiet as possible during the mule train's arrival. The Germans had patrols out and although we put out our own covering patrols, it was a time when we were very vulnerable to attack, and any unnecessary noise which might draw attention to ourselves and pinpoint positions of activity was frowned upon by authority.

Keith Robinson and I carried out a heavy box and hoisted it on to the pannier clips on the mule's left side. Unknown to us, the mule must have been standing on only three legs, its left rear leg being the one that was off the ground at the time. When it took the weight of the box, it naturally banged down its rear leg to maintain its balance. Unfortunately, Keith's foot was directly underneath that particular spot, and the full weight of a quarter of a mule plus the additional weight of the load drove his foot deep into the ground. Keith's yell of anguish was probably heard in Imola.

SSM Ambrose charged out of the house, turning the night air blue with his imprecations upon us for making so much racket, whilst Keith and I tried vainly to persuade the mule to lift its offending hoof. The harder we tugged and pushed, the more determined he was to stay put. Apparently, mules have a well-documented reputation for being stubborn in this fashion. Eventually four of us were pushing and pulling at the idiotic animal, but all to no effect. Mule and Keith remained welded to the earth.

Finally, since we could think of no other solution, I went in search of the muleteer and found him sipping a cup of tea in the house. I explained to him the difficulty we were experiencing so he came outside, wandered over to his charge, whispered something (probably endearing) into the mule's long ear and the beast promptly and obligingly stepped forward.

Released at last, Keith hobbled off to nurse his swollen toes, while we were left feeling rather exhausted by the whole affair, though principally from the effort of suppressing our laughter rather than from wrestling with the mule.

It is such seemingly trivial incidents which help to keep one sane in an otherwise insane environment. The ability to find amusement in small things is perhaps the mind's antidote to the general misery of war. Keith, however, was not in the market for philosophical musings and was distinctly miffed that we found the incident at all funny.

★★★★★★

At about 11:00hrs the following morning we were the target of an enormous 'stonk', most of which fell on and around our house. I spent the time standing in the doorway of the wireless room, gambling that if the house came down, the strength of the lintel would protect me to some extent. Eventually the shelling stopped and we inspected the damage. Through a door leading out of the wireless room was my bedroom. I peered in. My bed was buried beneath a mound of rubble, and with it the remains of four bottles of beer which I had saved for a small farewell drink before we left. Where the opposite wall had been I now had a superb view of the German positions on the opposite ridge. I unearthed what I could salvage of my bedding and moved it into the wireless room where I later spent a disturbed night.

The next day we all went about a little more carefully, not only because of the previous day's bombardment, but also because when you are about to be relieved you suddenly become aware of the dangers under which you have been living. How terrible it would be to succumb now, just when relief was in sight. Somehow the long day eventually came to a close. Evidently deciding that he had caused us enough discomfort, Jerry left us alone for most of the day, with only a few sporadic mortar bombs from his direction breaking the silence.

Eventually darkness fell and 'C' Squadron arrived to take over. One feels a tremendous affection for the relieving troops. "Good old 'C' Squadron! Come on in! Here's the telephone exchange, there's the wireless. Jerry's over there. Hope you have a pleasant eight days. We'll be off then. *Ciao!*"

Down the hill, along the poor second-class road back to Casola and aboard the waiting trucks. We were going back to Antella. 'A' Squadron had moved from there into Casola to act as village defence and await their turn for front line duty.

Back at Antella, we cleaned up, drew some pay, had a couple of trips into Florence and then prepared for our return to Casola Valsenio. After just over a week we were back there, billeted in a tall, shell-pocked three-storey house fronting the road. As usual, I was on the top floor from where, through a glassless window, I could see part of the mountain which we had recently left. There were about eight of us sharing this room as it was reasonably spacious.

Our duty in the village was simple. We were to defend it in the event of an enemy attack penetrating the forward position. My role was now that of No 1 on a Bren gun, which was sold to me as the most important position on the team, entrusted as I was with the actual firing of the gun. This was an honour I felt I would have gladly foregone since it meant I had to carry the damned thing around with me. It weighed at least six times as much as the Tommy gun I had been using and I was to come to roundly hate it. Happily, it was never necessary for me to actually use it in anger.

Across the river was a considerable mass of mountainside. The feature facing our house was given the code name 'Beef' and was the position that our troop would occupy in the event of an attack on the village. We carried out a dress rehearsal of occupying this position which took up a considerable part of the day and which left me with aching arms and shoulders as a result of my having to heft the Bren gun up and down the mountain.

Once on top of the vantage point, the view of the surrounding country was fantastic, and it illustrated yet again how readily the Germans had been able to frustrate our advance. It was as obvious to us (as it clearly was to the enemy) that positions like this could be defended by one man and a dog since they afforded wonderful observation of movements in the valley below, thus enabling shell and mortar fire to be directed with great accuracy on to any unfortunate attackers who would be in view almost irrespective of where they were in the landscape.

★★★★★★

Casola was under shellfire and one afternoon, just after our midday meal we were lying on our beds, reading, when a series of crashes announced the arrival of a routine 'stonk' directed on to our area. One shell hit the roof next to our room and there was a general stampede to the stairs and an exit to comparative safety.

As had become my wont, I was moving with considerable speed and as I made the turn out of the room on to the landing, my hobnailed boots slid on the stone surface and I crashed to the floor. I put out my right hand to break my fall and my wrist took the full force of my body weight as it hit the angle of floor and wall. The pain was excruciating. I sat in one of the ground floor rooms all afternoon nursing the aching joint, which seemed to become more painful as the day wore on. Eventually I was persuaded to visit the MI Room across the road, which was under the care of a South African Medical Officer. When I arrived he was seeing another patient in his office, so I sat on a chair to wait. Almost immediately the door opened and two men entered, supporting an Italian soldier, a member of 'F' Recce, an Italian commando style group. Where his right foot should have been was a bloody stump. I left immediately.

How could I waste an M.O's time with a sore wrist when there was someone with an injury like that requiring attention? I never went back and my wrist was never treated. It gradually improved, but has been a problem throughout my subsequent life. It was X-rayed at Stockport Infirmary in 1947 and was shown to have been broken, but I was advised against an operation to rectify the condition on the grounds that the procedure might make matters worse.

★★★★★★

At the end of February, we were told that we were to hand over to the Grado Assault Battalion of the highly regarded San Marco Regiment, a unit composed of Italian naval personnel. In fact, this regiment are the marines of the Italian Navy. Their signal officer was an ex-submarine commander. The unit could trace is history back to the early 18th century. It had fought in North Africa with such prowess that the German general, von Arnim described them as 'the best soldiers I ever commanded'. Many members of the San Marco Regiment joined the Allies to fight the Germans, but one unit of marines, the Caorle Battalion of the Carlotto Regiment, fought with the Axis forces until the end of the war.

★★★★★★

Whilst we were in the front line we had had some contact with the aforementioned 'F' Recce (1st Recce Squadron 'F'—members of an elite Italian parachute regiment serving with the Allies). One afternoon Major Watson visited their positions, which were along our ridge to the right. In the early evening he came back, rather pale, and I could swear, shaking slightly. He ordered the rum ration to be broken out and told us in hushed tones of his experience. Apparently their positions were festooned with wires from which were suspended booby-trapped grenades. What was worse, whenever one of them went outside for any reason, he set a further booby-trap but neglected to tell anyone.

They also regularly played football in full view of the Germans. Major Watson was convinced they were all mad and considered them a greater danger to us than they were to the Germans. There was no doubt, though, that they were very brave men and gave the lie to the unflattering reputation of Italian soldiers often have and which has been popularly fostered.

The final front line handover was made by 'A' Squadron, but not without incident. One of their protective patrols was intercepted by a German patrol and suffered casualties. Two of the four men in the patrol were wounded and the patrol leader, Corporal Watkinson was posted as missing. Several patrols were sent out to bring in the wounded and to search for Corporal Watkinson, but he was later reported to have been killed.

CHAPTER 14

The Final Battle

We arrived back in Antella just before midnight on the 3rd of March to be greeted by news that we would soon be on our way to the Adriatic coast. Could this be the final push we wondered?

We left Antella at 05:30hrs on the 8th of March 1945 and arrived at Pesaro at 14:00hrs. This was to be our home for the next month. Pesaro was a small seaside town some thirty miles back from the battlefront on the River Senio. It was pleasant, if old fashioned and carried some of the scars of war. We were allotted billets in a small estate of summer villas built in what might be described as the Victorian style. We now got our tanks back, and yes, they were the same ones we had handed over to the Forward Delivery Squadron at Osimo. We had already done a great deal of work on them, but were to spend a lot more time improving them even further.

There were signs to be painted on, guns to be taken out of preservation and in our case, fitting of wireless sets. We were the spare rear link tank, which meant having two No. 19 sets fitted, also a No. 38 set in a box welded to the rear of the tank for communications with the infantry.

★★★★★★

One matter which occupied our minds considerably was protection against *panzerfausts*, the German equivalent of the bazooka, though much simpler, lighter and a disposable 'one shot only', one-metre long weapon. Inexpensive to produce and designed to be carried and fired by a single soldier who had no

151

need to be a specialist, these weapons carried an anti-tank high explosive warhead. The fact that these things packed real killing potential and that they were out there in large quantities was obviously a concern. Though we did not know it at the time the Germans had produced over 6,000,000 of them and later in the war they even developed one that featured a reloadable tube. The projectile from these weapons had a fairly slow flight and did not depend on speed to penetrate armour. Experiments had shown that if the missile could be exploded before it came into contact with the tank's armour, even an inch or so away, its effect would be dissipated in the air. Everyone had his own theory as to the best method of protection. We opted for track plates welded on to the most vulnerable parts of the tank. We heard that in other squadrons wire netting was used. When the tanks were camouflaged the combined visual effect of these measures was bizarre to behold.

★★★★★★

My recollection of our stay in Pesaro is of an uneventful few weeks spent in rehearsals of future operations both with tanks and with the aid of sand tables. We managed to fit in several ENSA shows and a visit to a football match between 8th Army and a select touring all Army XI which contained several well-known players from pre-war days. Our 8th Army team had at inside-left Tom Finney, who was a tank crew member with the 9th Lancers, having renounced the opportunity of a cushy war in the Army Physical Training Corps. He was greatly respected for this and it is difficult, even today, to find an ex-tankman who does not consider him the model sportsman.

It was here at Pesaro that we were introduced to the delights of Asti Spumante. Corporal Bill Antinck, our barman, discovered a vast quantity of it at a knock-down price, and for weeks we drank it like tea. Fortunately, it has a fairly low alcohol content, thus reducing the danger of hangovers, and we found it an ideal drink at the end of a warm spring day.

The Po valley, in which we would be operating in the future, was far from being ideal tank country. The fields were long and narrow, sometimes three or four hundred yards long and only about thirty yards wide. They were separated by vines and olives and visibility was very restricted. Other tank obstacles were provided by the Po irrigation system which in addition to canals of varying size had flood banks ten to twenty feet high.

To assist us in our task, it was decided to convert our Reconnaissance Troop, which was mounted in Honey tanks (the Stuart tank, minus turret) and always called the Honey Troop, into a Pioneer troop. They were immediately set on training to lift mines, remove demolitions and generally facilitate the progress of the fighting tanks. We were also joined here by the infantry unit with whom we were to work during the coming operations—the 1st Battalion King's Royal Rifle Corps, and joint exercises were duly carried out.

Towards the end of our stay in Pesaro, the tempo quickened; final exercises, both TEWTs (Tactical Exercise without Troops) and sand-table demonstrations, were held and we were put in the picture regarding our future role and proposed tactics by the squadron leader. One feature of the Second World War was the way in which everyone was kept informed of the situation and of future plans, unlike World War I when the ordinary soldier was expected to risk his life without a clue as to what was going on.

On the 7th of April 1945, the 16th/5th Lancers moved to Cesena, about thirty miles north west of Pesaro, on Highway 9 and some eight miles from the sea, and about three days later the C.O. went through the plan for our new offensive with all tank crews.

★★★★★★

The 8th Army front line ran along the River Senio from the south west corner of Lake Comacchio across the main Bologna road to Casola Valsenio. From there the 5th Army carried the line westward to the Tyrrhenian Sea. Facing the 5th and 8th Armies were 23 German and 4 Italian divisions. They were well equipped for static defence and included a force of Tiger and Panther tanks armed with the dreaded 88mm 'flak' guns. A hit from one of these guns would penetrate our armour with devastating results. Although much depleted, the Allied armies had seven armoured brigades and were consequently much more mobile, and also enjoyed a high degree of air superiority.

There were apparently two possible routes for us to take but options were left open at this point. These routes were:—

1. Over the River Reno and along the south western shore of Lake Comacchio, up a narrow neck of land called the Argenta Gap.

2. South west of the flooded area parallel to Highway 9.
On the evening of the 9th of April, the 56th and 78th Divisions kicked off towards the Argenta Gap. The New Zealanders, Indians and Poles attacked the River Senio crossings and headed up the Bologna road. We waited to hear which route we were to follow.

★★★★★★

Late that evening we were informed that all tank tracks were to be fitted with platypus grousers. This was a device which doubled the width of the tracks and improved the performance of the tank over open country by providing enhanced traction. Each tank had 180 track plates, each of which had to have a grouser separately screwed on. It was the most fiddling, nail-breaking, finger-trapping job imaginable and took us three days and two nights, working under lights, to complete it. The air above Cesena was blue with the torrent of four-letter words. Eventually everyone was finished and the tanks looked very impressive, as the grousers stuck out like the knives on the Ancient Britons' war chariots.

The infantry was doing well, but going very slowly and we still waited to hear our fate. On the 14th we moved nearer the front to a concentration area in fields by the village of Lugo. Keith had had an immense stroke of luck whilst we were at Cesena. He was chosen to take a month's leave in the UK and went off to Naples to embark. We were green with envy. This was obviously going to be the last battle of the war and he was guaranteed to miss it. For Keith there would now be no chance of stopping a bullet or shell at the last hurdle. He had, of course, earned his remission because he had gone to war with the regiment in 1942 and had been in every action since that time. We promised to win the war without him and welcomed Joe McWalter into our tank as our replacement driver. Joe was a good friend of mine, and if we were to lose Keith we could not have wished for a better replacement. A Birmingham 'bobby' in civilian life, he was totally unflappable and a first class driver into the bargain.

★★★★★★

In our concentration area we met up with a lot of our old friends—the 1st Kings Royal Rifle Corps, 'C' Battery 12th Royal Horse Artillery, 111th Battery 72nd Anti-Tank Regt, 165th Light Field Ambulance, 8th Field Squadron Royal Engineers, and 'A' Squadron Derbyshire Yeomanry.

The weather was perfect—sunny and warm and the corn was six inches high. It seemed a pity we had to spoil it all.

On the 18th of April we woke to the news that our fate was settled. The selected route was going to be through the Argenta Gap. We left Lugo at 15:00hrs and after a very dusty drive harboured at 18:00hrs in some fields directly behind the leading units of 78th Division.

We were to lead the advance through the Argenta Gap. Oh, goody! This was not the best news.

We went to bed early but I could not sleep. I wondered if my luck was going to run out—after all, I had been in every action since we landed, with the exception of the battle of Second Mint-urno, and thus far had not collected so much as a scratch, apart from my wrist injury caused by an accident and a lump taken out of my leg during an involuntary descent through the turret hatch. What rotten luck it would now be if I should be killed or badly wounded right at the end of hostilities! I wondered how many of the men around me, in all the units crammed into the concentration area waiting for the off were entertaining the same thoughts. The answer was almost certainly all of them and there was no doubt that these concerns were also keeping each one of them awake on this night before battle.

Eventually I dropped off to sleep, but was awakened at 05:00 to face a hearty breakfast of tinned bacon, baked beans, bread and hot sweet tea. As this might well be the last food we would have before nightfall it was wise to stoke up one's personal engine.

I checked the squadron net on my wireless—the Squadron Rear Link set was playing up again, so we were in the first team. I frequently suspected that Captain Bull deliberately sabotaged his wireless sets so that he could hand over to us and go 'swanning' off to where something interesting was taking place.

At 08:00hrs on the 19th, we set off up the road towards the Argenta Gap. Although we did not know it at the time, the 16th/5th Lancers had just five more days of action in the Second World War.

The road was crowded with moving artillery pieces, with the Engineers in their huge bridging lorries, and with ammunition and fuel lorries all of them crawling northwards. Above us we could see the reassuring sight of our fighter planes patrolling the sky ready when called upon to protect the advance.

Just after mid-day we left the road and halted in the fields around Boccaleone. This proved to be a very temporary halt and we were soon off again in company with our KRRC partners. We were to head for a start line just beyond Il Trombone, from where we were to seize two crossings over a canalised tributary of the River Reno called the Po Morte Di Primaro. These two crossings, one called Traghetto and the other a bridge half a mile further north were about three and a half miles beyond the start point.

The start point was in some orchards and olive groves and it was soon apparent that the platypus grousers on our tanks as they ploughed up the track were making life very difficult for the wheeled vehicles of 1st KRRC which attempted to follow them. Orders were given for the infantry to transfer to our tanks, which was a precarious position for them to be as by now we were coming under intermittent shellfire.

We were considerably confused and not a little annoyed to discover that the enemy was holding some buildings actually on the start line, and that it also held the watercourse between Il Trombone and Traghetto.

This was a serious situation. We had ordered a strike of our fighter-bombers aircraft on Traghetto at 16:00hrs and it now looked as if we would not get there in time to take advantage of the damage they would inflict. Our infantry dismounted from our hulls and together we set off at 15:30hrs. We had three and a half miles to cover and just half an hour to do it in. We were never in with a chance of arriving in the time we had for the task. The countryside was criss-crossed with lines of vines and olive trees Every now and then there was a dyke between eight and twelve feet wide to negotiate. Furthermore, within no more than fifty yards from the point where we began the advance we ran into hidden enemy posts which opened fire upon us with small arms. This, naturally, slowed up the infantry, who were advancing on foot parallel to our flanks and also made it necessary for the tanks to 'close down,' (close hatches and navigate by periscope).

Our advance had not proceeded more than half a mile when our fighter-bombers made their attack on cue. The artillery concentration stopped and the guns gave direct support. In this fashion we made slow progress and as darkness began to fall, 'B' Squadron was about a mile from its bridge. Furthermore, we were unreachable by our supply echelon as a bridge over the River Reno had been blown up. Fortunately, supplies of ammunition and fuel were brought forward to us by our Honey tanks. I spent an hour carrying fuel and ammunition across an enormous bumpy field. The Sappers did a wonderful job in that between 02:00hrs and 06:00hrs they erected seventy feet of Bailey bridge and so this ensured the unimpeded transfer of future supplies.

We were told that the Traghetto Gap was strongly held and that the divisional commander had decided that an attempt at the crossing should be made by a combined force of 'B' Squadron, 16th/5th Lancers and 'B' Company 1st KRRC, supported by a heavy artillery concentration.

At first light, unshaven, unwashed and with only a mug of tea and some bully beef and army biscuits inside us we moved off once again. We arrived at our bridge at 08:30hrs only to find it destroyed before us, the river was unable to be forded at this point and that there was enemy infantry in defensive positions on both levees. However, Lieutenant Brooke's troop managed to get up on the nearest levee and supported a successful crossing by 'B' Company. By 09:30hrs we were in control of the crossing.

We were now told to leave the riflemen where they were and to push on as fast as possible to gain control of the Canale Cembaline from Marrara to Segni. We were stuck for some time at the Traghetto crossing and were subjected to very heavy shelling there. Our Sherman was hit twice by high explosive shells but thankfully suffered no severe damage.

Throughout all of this time, in my role as Rear Link, I had to contact every tank in the squadron to ascertain their requirements for the following day in respect of rations, fuel, ammunition and spare parts for the tank. All these individual amounts had to be consolidated into a single squadron indent, then put into code and transmitted to the regiment. This is not a difficult task when performed seated at a desk, but to do it perched on a tiny seat in a crowded turret within a swaying, rolling tank, to the more than distracting accompaniment of what sounds like an iron foundry working at full capacity immediately outside the tank does present some challenges. After much shouting and a fair amount of repetition combined with a short foray into Morse Code, I got the message through. I had only just finished when an airburst exploded overhead and a sizeable piece of shrapnel scorched past my head and embedded itself in my right-hand wireless set. I tested the set, but found that miraculously the missile had not hit anything vital and it still worked.

In view of the difficulties experienced in sending this indent, I awaited the night's deliveries with great trepidation, but to my relief everything was delivered as per order.

★★★★★★

The army is often derided, but it mostly gets the important things right. Take troop movements as an example. Several times during the Italian campaign our entire division moved from one side of the country to the other, but on far more occasions it moved a mere thirty or forty miles. This is the equivalent of packing up a small town, (say Hyde, where I came from), and moving it with all its inhabitants and chattels and having it re-established thirty miles away, with everyone settled in by the end of the day and ready to recommence business, all without anyone having missed a meal.

★★★★★★

Once over the crossing, we were ordered to push on alone as 'A' Squadron were held up by anti-tank fire at Cortilli. Progress was slow but steady, but as we advanced across some very open, bare country we came under fire from some enemy self-propelled guns in farm buildings. I looked on in horror as the tanks on either side of us were knocked out and waited, heart thumping, for our turn to be hit. Bert Ambrose ordered Joe to reverse the Sherman; that accomplished we took cover behind two of the thinnest, most unprepossessing trees I have ever seen. Surely, this was no good! However, for some reason the enemy gun lost interest in us and switched to other targets so we got away with it.

In 5th Troop, 'Mush' Berry, a co-driver, was decapitated by one of the armour-piercing shells and in total we lost five tanks knocked out and several others damaged but driveable in this scrap. An air strike was called in from the 'Cab Rank' system and almost immediately the self-propelled guns were blasted out of existence by well-aimed rockets delivered by the responding aircraft. The 'Cab Rank' system consisted of a number of fighter-bombers circling around the battle area. On request to the R.A.F Liaison Officer at Brigade H.Q, giving a map reference, three or more fighter-bombers were diverted to deal with the nuisance.

One of the tanks knocked out was commanded by Lieutenant Brooke. The crew bailed out and took cover in a ditch, but each time they tried to make a run for it to the rear, they came under heavy enemy small arms fire. At considerable risk to himself, Reg Robinson climbed back into the tank and put down a number of smoke shells from the 2-inch mortar. Under the cover of the smokescreen the crew were then able to make their escape. Reg was wounded in this action and was later awarded the Military Medal for his bravery.

As darkness fell, we harboured at the scene of our ordeal. After we had replenished our supplies, to my displeasure I was detailed to do guard duty, something which I normally escaped in favour of wireless watch. I spent a most unpleasant hour lying in the long damp grass and being at one point startled by stealthy figures moving up a sunken road just below me. Were they Germans? Should I challenge, fire, or what? It was a great relief at last to hear indistinct but unmistakeably English voices. These were obviously the riflemen who were coming up to dig in ahead of us. On the 21st we moved forward to the Cembaline Canal and managed to get out heads down by midnight.

At 04:30hrs on the 22nd of April we were given fresh orders to push on to Bondeno and again we gave our comrades in the KRRC a lift into action on our tanks. This was tough going—we made good time for about eight miles to the village of Coronella, but there we met fierce resistance. We were fired at by practically everything the enemy had in its arsenal which included a particularly narrow escape from a hit by the German equivalent of a bazooka which they called the *panzershreck*.

More parochially perhaps, the afternoon was singular for me by a fierce argument I had in the tank with Bert Ambrose. Very soon after the 'bazooka' incident we were dealing with attacks by anti-tank infantry who were positioned in the ditches all around us. We were also firing shells into a nearby house occupied by more German infantry who were taking a heavy toll of the infantrymen of the King's Royal Rifle Corps.

I was working flat-out at this time. The temperature outside the tank was in the high 80s F, inside the tank it was at least 100°. I was dressed in denim overalls, over the top of which I wore a tank suit, a marvellous contraption with countless useful features, such as pockets and zips everywhere and which when removed and with zips suitably realigned, converted to a sleeping bag. This form of dress was as per orders; very suitable for chilly early mornings but akin being in a sauna in the middle of the day. This constituted a handicap in itself, but in addition I was festooned in headsets for the No. 19 set, and engaged in keeping wireless watch back to regiment.

As we were firing both the 105mm gun and the .30 Browning turret-mounted machine gun, I was also fully occupied in keeping them loaded and free from stoppages. The shells for the 105mm were located in clips around the turret walls. The remainder were kept under the turret floor. I had used all the shells which had been stored around the turret wall and now had to start drawing on the under-floor stock.

The turret, of course, revolves actuated by an electric switch in the form of a pistol-grip, and operated by the gunner. The top floor of the turret is really only a half-floor, enabling access to the lower floor and ammunition chambers. As we were engaging several targets, the turret was swinging from side to side and I could not get at the ammunition.

Even when I could, the effort required to lift a 33lb shell plus case from below floor level and heave it up into the breech was having its effect on my stamina. So when Bert yelled down to enquire what the ——— I was doing down there and did I want us to be brewed up through my idleness, years of discipline deserted me and for about a minute I told him what I thought about him, his fire orders and his general command of the tank.

I suppose in the modern world this outburst would be called being stressed-out. I was so exhausted, harassed and generally bloody-minded that I honestly couldn't have cared less if the anti-tank guns had finished us. When I had calmed down, I began to wonder what would happen. Such insubordination, and to a warrant officer renowned for his disciplinary zeal, would be surely severely punished. In fact, even a court martial was not out of the question. Surprisingly, Bert never referred to the incident ever again. Once we had dealt with the enemy posts he resumed normal conversation as though nothing had happened.

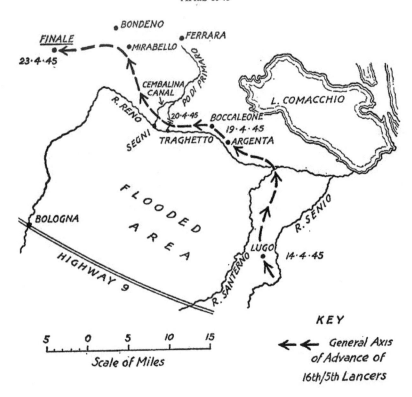

ITALY—THE LAST PHASE

APRIL 1945

BONDENO

FINALE
23·4·45

MIRABELLO

FERRARA

PO DI PRIMARO

CEMBALINA
CANAL

R. RENO

SEGNI

20·4·45

L. COMACCHIO

BOCCALEONE
19·4·45

TRAGHETTO

ARGENTA

BOLOGNA

F L O O D E D

A R E A

R. SENIO

HIGHWAY 9

R. SANTERNO

LUGO

14·4·45

5   0   5   10   15

Scale of Miles

KEY

← ← General Axis
of Advance of
16th/5th Lancers

CHAPTER 15

The Last Angry Shots

This was a particularly hectic action for the whole troop and as we halted to regroup, we felt physically and emotionally drained. Suddenly we were greeted by a Pathe News cinema newsreel camera crew. They explained that they had seen the battle, but could not get their cameras set up in time to film whilst it was actually taking place. So they asked us, to our astonishment, if we would mind doing it again, so they could film a re-enactment. I expected the Squadron Leader to send them packing, but surprisingly he agreed, so we closed down the hatches, loaded our guns and blazed off at nothing in particular for about five minutes, after which the film crew thanked us profusely for our cooperation and departed.

By the end of the day we had taken 450 enemy prisoners. We had fought our way to the rear of the main German forces and their only hope to extricate themselves was to cross the River Po and organise some defence behind the northern bank. That night we harboured in a most unhealthy place. We had scarcely begun to start maintenance when we came under heavy fire from mortars across the valley. This enemy fire was accurate and seriously interfered with our work. Then we discovered we could see the flashes as the mortars were fired; about ten seconds later the shells arrived. I appointed myself lookout and stood on the turret. Whilst the others were filling up with petrol and cleaning the gun, I kept my eyes trained on the spot where the mortars were situated.

As soon as I saw the flashes, I gave the word and we all quite sedately climbed into the tank, shut down the hatches and waited for the crash of the bombs. Then we got out again and carried on with our work. This was a tedious procedure, but a safe and effective way of ensuring we could get on with the routine of our regular duties. On reflection, what is most peculiar is that the irritation of these disruptions was a hail of lethal explosive and our solution for accommodating it had become so pragmatic. Our sleep that night, such as it was, was punctuated by the explosions of shells and mortar bombs and so we felt very weary as we prepared to move off in the following morning.

We had an early start, 05:00hrs, and our objective was Finale, an appropriate name as it happened. Looking at my diary entry for that day I see it says only the following:—

Best day yet. Still bags of action, but took huge total of prisoners and linked up with 6th South African Armoured Division and Americans. Big bag of enemy transport and stores. Reached Finale.

Not what one would call deathless prose, but then I never fancied myself as a war correspondent.

The country was open to begin with but for greater speed we stuck to the road. A few months earlier we would have been wary of running into a trap, but the Germans appeared to be on the run and we were told that risks must be taken. The tanks of 'B' Squadron were leading, and we made good progress until we reached a point within a mile of Finale, where upon the country became very enclosed and we were fired on by both enemy tanks and guns. Our leading tanks began to return the fire and I heard on the wireless that they had knocked out two Panthers and two 75mm assault guns. Almost immediately we caught up with a large number of enemy troops travelling in lorries and these were shot up.

We arrived at the Panaro bridge in Finale just as the head of the enemy column was arriving from another direction, and immediately opened fire upon it. The following few minutes brought an almost indescribable scene of confusion and slaughter. The German vehicles were jammed nose to tail and were a sitting target for us-many caught fire, some exploded and hundreds of German troops were caught in the concentrated fire from our tanks as they tried to escape from the burning vehicles. The main bridge had been blown but a light trestle-type bridge was still surviving.

The villagers poured out of their houses and climbed aboard our tanks, offering flagons of wine and baskets of fruit. All around me beaming tank crews were slowly submerging in a sea of *vino*, yet I steadfastly refused even a drop. This may well be received with incredulity by the reader, but I had long ago made a decision not to indulge in alcohol when in action. I knew it slowed down my reactions and promoted complacency and carelessness and I determined that if I did get killed I was not going to contribute to the event by negligence. There would be ample time to celebrate when the war was over.

Just at this point, a sad incident occurred which demonstrated the fact that the war still had a sting in its tail. As we in 'B' Squadron were halted at the river, our CO, Lieutenant Colonel Smyly joined up with the CO of the 1st KRRC, Lieutenant Colonel Hope, and set off to meet us in the command Honey tank. When the tank stopped momentarily, a German sniper fired and hit Colonel Hope. Corporal Waring, the tank commander, jumped out of the turret to get to the first aid box to assist Colonel Hope when he too was shot by this sniper and killed instantly. Colonel Hope was taken back for treatment but later died of his wounds.

The 16th/5th Lancers Regimental history in referring to this incident says that the sniper, who was dressed in civilian clothes, was later taken prisoner by the KRRC in a sweep of the area. My information which came from the Honey Troop itself, differs from the official version and according to them what actually happened was that the surviving members of the crew leapt out of their Honey and cornered the sniper, who dropped his rifle and raised his hands, at which point he received the contents of a full magazine from a Thomson sub-machine gun. Since I did not witness any of these events personally, the reader is at liberty to select the version that seems most plausible.

At one point along the road we thought we had come under fire from a German tank unit on our left flank, and there was an exchange of armour-piercing shells before a forceful and expletive-ridden message in a South African accent came through which advised us to desist our fire forthwith. Unknown to us, the 11th South African Armoured Brigade, which was within the US 5th Army, had come up on our left and we, with potentially tragic consequences, had mistaken them for the enemy.

Another typical example of the confusion which was rampant on this day was the casual meeting that someone had with an American officer who informed our regimental HQ that an American infantry division was about to put in an attack on our own rear. This attack, which was to be preceded by a creeping artillery barrage was only just stopped in time, by a liaison officer of the 17th/21st Lancers who happened to arrive at the American division's HQ just before the artillery programme was due to start. The consequences, had the situation not been remedied in the nick of time, would have been catastrophic for us.

We watched the Americans cross the river in line abreast, a perfect target if any German machine-gunners had been present, and later, as the light began to fail we withdrew under orders to our previous night's harbour. This time there was no dodging of mortar bombs; in fact, we lit fires in the open to cook our food and sat around into the night smoking and yarning. We were informed later that our 'score' for that day was 100 enemy killed, 1000 enemy taken prisoner, 160 lorries, various half-tracks, anti-aircraft guns, field guns, mortars and machine guns destroyed together with a Tiger tank which had stalked us for about an hour during the morning. Three Mark IV Panther tanks were also all destroyed.

★★★★★★

Before we went to bed we were told that we would have two days' rest while measures were taken to get tanks across the River Po, (which was roughly the same width as the River Thames at Westminster Bridge), but it was not to be. The crossing of the Po and the Adige Rivers was carried out by the two infantry brigades of the 6th Armoured Division—the 1st Guards Brigade and the 61st Lorried Infantry Brigade, together with the Derbyshire Yeomanry, 12th Lancers and 2nd New Zealand Division.

Again, my diary shows that we were resting on the 24th, 25th, 26th, 27th, and 28th of April. The entry for the 27th mentions that we were standing by to cross the Po; that for the 28th, a Saturday, refers to 'good news from the front'.

★★★★★★

On Sunday the 29th, we moved to the village of Vigarano, where we parked our tanks on the main street and moved into some empty houses alongside of them. That night, three of us went for a walk around the village and called by chance at a house to enquire whether they had any wine to sell in exchange for cigarettes. Without any hesitation the occupants invited us into their home and regaled us freely with the white wine of the region. The house was owned by a married couple in their early fifties who had two stunningly attractive daughters. Their father owned a small factory in Milan, but the family had been caught up in the fighting and cut off here in Vigarano, where they owned this weekend holiday cottage. None of the family could speak English and our Italian was not sufficient to sustain a conversation, but we discovered that the father and I could speak reasonable French. My own conversation in that language was a little bit rusty, even though I had achieved a distinction in my School Certificate French examination paper some six years previously.

However, as the evening wore on and the wine flowed, communication improved, our host brought out an accordion and I retained sufficient expertise to play it and accompany the family and my comrades in various internationally-known numbers including '*Lili Marlene*' rendered in its suitably sanitised version, of course.

By the time the evening came to a close, I had established a definite rapport with one of the daughters, and as we left we promised to return the following evening bearing gifts of corned beef, tinned fruit and cigarettes as our contribution to the entertainment. My new friend, Carla, promised to show me around the grounds, although accompanied by the traditional Italian chaperone system, so I did not hold my breath as to any possibility of a romantic interlude. Nevertheless, it was nice to have some civilised company (particularly female) for a change, and so we all looked forward with anticipation to the following evening.

The next morning found me making up a parcel of 'goodies' to take to our new friends that evening when a message arrived putting us on two hours' notice to move. Almost immediately we were ordered to get under way. Typically, of my luck, I had been sitting in a field for five days doing nothing, then as soon as we found some pleasant diversion, off we went again.

This time we moved to an olive tree grove by a farmhouse on the banks of the River Po. For two days we languished there and then on the 2nd of May we at last received the wonderful news that an armistice had been signed and the war in Italy was over.

★★★★★★

This is the point at which I started these reminiscences, and although I had intended that they should end with the ending of the war, second thoughts suggested that my return to normal civilian life might be a more suitable closure. I ask readers to forgive me for indulging myself further with a retrospective excursion into the immediate post-war world.

CHAPTER 16

After the War was Over

On the 3rd of May, Colonel Dennis Smyly addressed us and explained that our future role would be occupational duties, probably in Austria, and we would be equipped with armoured cars. We would be staying where we were until at least the 21st of May. We managed the occasional celebration, but the real festivities were put on hold until VE Day. Our war in Italy was over, but the Germans were still holding out in their own country and it was not until the 8th of May that VE Day (Victory in Europe) was declared. The regiment really went to town with a cocktail party in the Officers' Mess and smoking concerts in each squadron.

Where was I whilst all this jollity was taking place? On Regimental Guard, of course. Bad enough luck in its own right, one may imagine, but nearby was a huge ammunition dump and some inebriate from a neighbouring unit managed to set fire to it, which sent all the unfortunate sentries to ground whilst all kinds of lethal metallic items fell to earth around us. I couldn't help feeling that it would be just my luck to survive the war and be killed during the peace celebrations. Happily, we all survived and the experience made us forget our annoyance at missing the formal celebrations.

The following day, the 9th, we attended a Brigade Thanksgiving Service and the next two days saw us hard at work cleaning and servicing the tanks prior to handing them over to their new charges. The transfer was duly made and we took delivery of Staghound armoured cars, huge six-wheeled monsters with pre–selector gearboxes and power steering capability at the driver's discretion if he felt the conditions required it. Keith had by this time returned from leave and resumed his position as our driver.

✶✶✶✶✶✶

The Staghound was an American made armoured car from Chevrolet armed with a 37mm gun in a rotating turret supported by a coaxial machine gun and a bow mounted machine gun. It carried a crew of five and had armour which was between 9mm to 42mm thick. Weighing nearly 14 tons this was an imposing vehicle that had a range of 450 miles and could travel at speeds up to 55mph. It saw some service in the Italian Campaign where the terrain was often open, but was considered too bulky for the war in northern Europe because its size made it unlikely to be able to manoeuvre freely through narrow urban streets.

The Staghounds of the 16th/5th Lancers sported 'crimped' pennants from their wireless aerials. Only this British cavalry regiment's pennant were crimped. This distinction came from the 16th Lancers side of the amalgamation of the two regiments and has its origins during the First Anglo–Sikh War in India. At the Battle of Aliwal in 1846 in the Punjab that regiment was so severely engaged that the lance pennants of the troopers, which had up to that time been a plain as every other lancer regiment, took on the appearance of having been crimped as a result of drying out after being drenched in enemy blood.

This is, of course, a grisly reminder of what war fought by cavalry armed with lances was actually like, but nevertheless, it was an outstanding victory for the regiment since its famous charge broke the 'square' (which was actually triangular in this instance) of the Sikh infantry of the Khalsa Army. Infantry squares were formed specifically to resist cavalry charges during this period so this was no mean achievement. To memorialise the battle that brought it so many encomiums the regiment had adopted the crimped pennant (now achieved by more conventional methods, naturally) since that time and celebrated, 'Aliwal Day' on the 28th of January every year. The tradition was carried

Staghound armoured cars

on into the 16th/5th Lancers.

★★★★★★

On the 26th of May at 06:00hrs, with our cars newly painted and with crimped pennants flying from the wireless aerials, we left the Po River valley for Klagenfurt in Austria. The journey took two days; the first night being spent at Tabina. The weather was atrocious, with continuous rain. We left early on the 27th and drove via Udine and Villach, reaching Klagenfurt at 14:30hrs. Our destination was a small village called Kuhnsdorf, about twenty-five miles from Klagenfurt. For the next few weeks we went out on daily patrols, visiting houses, rounding up Germans, especially SS personnel who had gone to ground, and collecting enemy equipment.

★★★★★★

As all the regiment was together more or less in the same place, the highly unpopular practice of mounting a Regimental Quarter Guard was reinstated. This was a real spit-and-polish 24-hour guard. I had been on one in Africa, but had been fortunate enough to be awarded the 'stick'. The 'stick' system rewarded the smartest man on parade by excusing him from the guard, and also reflected great glory on his squadron. As a previous 'stick man' I was expected to repeat the feat when I was named for the Quarter Guard at Kuhnsdorf. To this end, I was allowed to borrow the best equipment in the squadron—cross belts, main belt, gaiters—anything. I spent the day before the guard polishing and cleaning.

On the appointed day I was up at 05:30hrs, had an early breakfast and got dressed. On parade at 07:00hrs for the Orderly Sergeant's inspection, 07:15hrs for the Orderly Officer and SSM's inspection. Bert Ambrose looked at my KD trousers and pronounced my chances as nil. They were quite badly creased. They had been one piece of my equipment I had not checked! The reason for that was that they had been kept beneath my bottom blanket, the traditional method of producing a razor-sharp crease. Unfortunately, mine were newly issued and the residual creases must have been resistant to my body weight. However, there was nothing for it but to go, and hope for the best.

The Regimental parade was quite gruelling—lots of drill, marching and manoeuvring before the Duty Officer began his inspection. I concentrated on my bearing—an immaculate military poise, rock-stillness, my chest out to its maximum expansion—any advantage I could muster, in fact, to draw attention away from my horrible trousers. After an age the inspection was over; a muttered conversation, then the Regimental Sergeant Major tapped me on the shoulder. "Stick man," he murmured. On the command "Stick man fall out!" I marched off the parade ground and into the guard room with a great feeling of relief. I had upheld the honour of the squadron, and any involvement in the guard from now on would be restricted to driving around in a scout car or jeep, collecting food and tea urns from the cookhouse and delivering it to the guard. I waited for the guard mounting to be completed.

There was a great gaffe of some kind just at the crucial point where the old guard hands over to the relief. The RSM marched off and entered the guard room. He was an impressive figure six feet four inches tall and about three feet wide; he had joined us in 1943 from the Coldstream Guards and drill was his passion. Now, he was incandescent with rage. Ignoring me, he circled the room twice, roaring his annoyance, ripped off his beret, hurled it to the floor, jumped up and down on it and exited with a slam of the back door.

★★★★★★

In June, the 8th Army started a leave scheme. This entailed sending large numbers of troops home in lorries via transit camps in Italy, Austria, Germany and France. It came to pass that 'B' Squadron was chosen to set up the 6th Armoured Division camp at Weissenburg, near Neu Ulm. We left on the 7th of June and took over a very dilapidated old barracks, but with the assistance of 200 POWs to clean it up, we soon had it operating. Each afternoon about 800 men would arrive and we would direct them to their dormitories, feed them, serve them with drinks, get them up in the morning, give them breakfast and get them on the road at 08:00hrs. Then we would begin our task of preparing for the next batch later in the day. I had my own gang of POWs who I

173

bribed with extra rations to finish in record time.

It was hard work and I was not sorry when during the final two weeks of our stay I was drafted into the Squadron Office to help with an influx of paper work caused in part by the voting for the General Election. During our stint at this transit camp we were visited by General Charles Keightley. His arrival was delayed, and the guard of honour of which I was a member was standing in the sun for over two hours awaiting him. As we were dismissed after his inspection we were told that we would be required again to see him off in the morning. I booked an early call, but was wakened at 05:00hrs to be told that he had already gone, having declined a formal send-off. What a splendid chap he was!

After five weeks we handed over to another unit and left for our new quarters at Knittelfeld. On the way back, between Augsburg and Landsberg, our car was hit a glancing blow by an American truck travelling on the wrong side of the road, which damaged the steering and deposited us into a tree, with the two near side wheels overhanging a considerable drop. It took me a considerable time to extricate myself from the car, as an unwary move could have upset the balance and sent us plunging down the drop. Keith Robinson suffered a badly cut head and I had badly bruised ribs and various minor cuts.

No one else seemed to be hurt. Keith was taken to hospital, and the rest of us bedded down in an adjoining field. We survived for the next two days on eggs, black bread and butter traded for cigarettes at a nearby farm. Help eventually arrived and under the direction of Sergeant Davies, who was now our crew commander in the absence of Bert Ambrose, we transferred our kit and ourselves to scout cars and with an overnight stop at Vipiteno reached Knittelfeld late that night, bloody, as they say, but unbowed.

In September we handed in our Staghounds and took over tanks again. We were in a pleasant block of flats surrounded by fields, one of which we used for playing basketball. The only alcoholic drink available was brandy and by order of the squadron leader, Bill Antinck the mess corporal was only allowed to serve it in milk. The squadron's milk consumption rose to such heights that the milk supply ran out, and reluctantly we had to drink the brandy neat.

Regimental stables were set up and a riding school was held in the early mornings and evenings. We spent several happy days constructing a steeplechase course, which entitled us to stay for the meetings in case repairs were needed.

Back at Knittelfeld, I was consigned to the office as Norman Cox, the squadron clerk had gone on 'demob'. I was not overjoyed about this change of occupation, but with winter approaching an indoor job could have its advantages.

A Regimental School was established and from the existing personnel within the regiment instructors were found to teach joinery, carpentry, bricklaying, plumbing and house wiring. On the academic side, languages, art, music and typing (using civilian instructors) classes were held. An additional, and very popular class was motor engineering. These classes were offered to those people in early release groups. By this time, we were beginning to lose people to essential occupations—our policemen and building trade workers went quickly.

Large parties were sent out to lumber camps to fell trees, clean them and chop them into metre lengths, load them into lorries and transport them. This was to alleviate the hardships of the civil population. Skiing was a popular pastime and schools were set up at various mountain centres.

The high spot of 1945 for me was a month's UK leave granted in December, which meant I would be home for Christmas. I cannot remember a lot about this leave except that my parents were overjoyed to see me and I realised what a strain they had undergone for the past few years, knowing I was in a fighting unit and therefore in danger, and no doubt dreading the arrival of a telegram from the War Office.

When I left after Christmas my father was ill, and I was quite worried. He recovered, however, and I received the good news that he was fit once more in late January 1946. The journey back to Austria was horrendous. Our cross-channel boat was within sight of Calais harbour when fog came down and we were stuck at anchor for twelve hours. I was on deck and it froze hard that night. I was numb for about three days. The journey across Europe in an unheated tram with wooden seats was bad enough, but when we arrived in Villach, the whole camp was frozen up and we amused ourselves by attending every showing at the camp cinema. After four days of waiting to be picked up by regimental transport, four of us went AWOL and hitch-hiked back to our unit. We managed it in two lifts but I was surprised to find that 'B' Squadron was no longer at Knittelfeld, having moved to Strassburg, a little village in the Gurk valley. It reminded me of the old joke about the boy who came home from school one day to find his family had moved without telling him. However, I was reassured that I was still *persona grata* by the news that in my absence I had been promoted to the dizzy heights of lance-corporal.

I thoroughly enjoyed our stay at Strassburg. Our time there encompassed the snows of winter and glorious summer days (and a few spectacular thunderstorms). I was billeted at first in a house across from the Squadron Office, to which I returned reluctantly as clerk. The Squadron Other Ranks bar was open for only an hour each day, 19:00hrs to 20:00hrs and as a result saw some Herculean feats of drinking which was not surprising, since this was the only form of entertainment we had apart from the occasional sleigh ride.

With the spring came the award of my second stripe and a transfer from the office, which could not accommodate a full corporal. Instead I was given command of a troop of tanks, a measure of what the shortage of manpower had done to our establishment. Normally, a troop is commanded by a lieutenant, with a sergeant as No 2 and a corporal as No 3. Now I was leading a troop, with a lance-corporal and a senior trooper in the other two tanks. Fortunately, we never had to move! I spent each morning organising and running wireless-based schemes, fighting imaginary battles from out-of-date maps. The afternoons, though, were free and I spent them playing table tennis in the Corporals' Mess under the tutelage of 'Tug' Wilson, who was a qualified Sussex County table tennis coach. He had been on secondment to the Yugoslav partisans from the 27th Lancers and was quite mad.

In May the squadron sent representatives to the Victory March in London. Those selected included everyone who had been decorated and when it appeared that there was one more vacancy, the choice fell on the two remaining senior NCOs—myself and Bill Curd. There was no point of difference between us either in rank or service, so we were both summoned to Squadron Office and invited to toss a coin to decide who was to go. My usual luck persisted and I lost.

To add insult to injury, since Reg Robinson, who was the present clerk and a holder of the MM was going, I was told to take over Squadron Office. My protests that my rank exceeded the establishment fell on deaf ears. I handed over my tank troop and with ill grace moved back into the office.

One benefit accrued from the move, however. In retyping the leave roster, I ensured that my name headed the list of candidates with equal priority and within three weeks I was on my way to the UK. I had a splendid spring leave in spite of the fact that there was a beer famine at home, and took the opportunity to visit ICI and check on the availability of my job when my 'demob' eventually arrived.

On return from leave I expected to get my tank troop back but was appalled to be handed the poisoned chalice of the echelon. So many people had left that I was the most senior NCO available for a job which normally took a senior sergeant, under command of an officer. The echelon consisted of about twenty-five vehicles of assorted sizes and capabilities and was manned by a formidable collection of mainly old soldiers, most of whom had been together throughout the war, leavened by a few transferees from tank crews. They were a real handful to manage and I was grateful that things were fairly relaxed discipline-wise.

During the summer, 'B' Squadron left Strassburg and took up residence in several blocks of apartments on an estate in St Veit-an-der-Glan in Carinthia. In May, the regiment had received an invitation from the French armoured regiment, the 2nd Conde Dragoons to send a football team to play them at their HQ in the Tyrolean town of Schwartz, near Innsbruck. Although not a footballer, I was invited along to act as interpreter. My school-boy French was still proving useful! We were given wonderful hospitality and the match ended in a diplomatic 2-2 draw. The French CO was a Colonel Toulouse L'Autrec!

Once settled in at St Veit, we were delighted to hear that a return visit by the French was planned and again my services were required. I was excused all duties from Friday evening until Monday morning and made the most of it. The day of their arrival, the 17th August, was my 23rd birthday and I enjoyed the dinner on the first day. On the Sunday we had an eight-course lunch followed by the match, which the regiment won 4-0. A first class dinner and dance concluded the festivities, and after an evening spent with the French team in the Sergeants' Mess I woke up in a spare bed in the mess, having been put to bed by a 'burial party' led by Squadron Sergeant Major Davies, who had replaced SSM Ambrose, absent since January with a broken leg caused by a skiing accident.

★★★★★★

My transport troop was based at St Veit station, the vehicles being parked on the station forecourt, while I took over the sta-tionmaster's office as my operations centre. Just along the road was the fuel dump which also came under my control. As the issuing of fuel was a dirty and tedious job involving manually pumping out petrol and diesel fuel from 40-gallon drums into jerricans, to say nothing of the fact that it was over a quarter of a mile from my billet, I fell into the habit of handing over the keys to any driver needing fuel, asking him to help himself and bring the issue note for me to sign later. When the time came to hand over the stocks to audit in advance of a move, I was horrified to find myself 250 gallons short. I called all the drivers together and explained the situation.

I told them that they, or some of them at least, had got me into this mess, and I expected them to get me out of it. For the next two weeks they indented for double the amount neces-sary and took only half, falsified milometer readings and coasted downhill wherever possible to save fuel. By the time I handed

The footbal team in Austria

over the stocks, the books were in balance. I think it is safe for me to reveal this transgression after 52 years has elapsed.

★★★★★★

St Veit was a very pleasant posting. We opened our own restaurant, run by one of our own lads who had worked as a chef in a Lyons Corner House in 'civvy street' (civilian life), and we enjoyed some wonderful meals at ridiculous prices. It became routine to eat out every night and the takings supplemented squadron funds. The social life was good, too, at this time. We had numerous squadron dances and another advantage was that expanses of glorious countryside to explore and enjoy was within easy walking distance.

It was, therefore, with great sadness that we learned of an impending move to Tessendorf, near Klagenfurt. This hideous hutted camp brought the whole regiment together for the first time since Kuhnsdorf. I hated it from the very beginning and nothing occurred subsequently to induce me to change my opinion of this place up to the point the day I gratefully left it behind me forever.

I did have a welcome break, going for a month's course to the College of the Central Mediterranean at Spittal. There I studied commerce, accountancy and economics under a mixture of civilian and army instructors. I was given command of a barrack room full of Royal Irish Fusiliers who were being taught how to read and write. They spent their off-duty hours drinking and fighting, and on occasion firing guns at the windows. It was a hairy assignment and being guard commander in charge of six of these 'boyos' was a nightmare. On one such guard I was on my rounds, checking that everything was in order, when I stuck my head in the NAAFI. The scene was reminiscent of a Wild West saloon at its most riotous. Without much deliberation I decided that the best policy for all concerned would be to visit the other side of the camp until the *fracas* quietened down. The weather at Spittal was very cold and we were trudging around in a foot of snow.

My job back at Tessendorf was very unpleasant. The weather was so cold that holding a pen or pencil was an eerie sensation;

my fingers were so numb I could not control it and the results were nothing like the neat joined-up writing I had intended. There was no heating in the huts and the only warmth we had was obtained from holding a mug of tea. Furthermore, we were short of vehicles and the demands of the regiment for transport verged on the unreasonable.

To add to the misery, owing to a shortage of NCOs I was on guard duty almost every other night, and on Orderly Sergeant duties three times a week. The guard duties ranged from normal squadron guards to army stores and ammunition dumps, and once a very prestigious one on 8th Army HQ in Klagenfurt.

I was having considerable trouble, too, from our recent re-cruits from the Royal Gloucestershire Hussars. The first intake had joined us at St Veit and immediately posted their intention of being a pain in the neck. They had come from the UK on dis-bandment of their regiment and brought with them a peacetime regimentation which fitted ill with our more relaxed regime. I had many run-ins with their NCOs and was convinced that this was the way our soldiering was to go now that peacetime was upon us.

It was at this time that I was approached by the Squadron Leader, Major Johnson and other officers to consider signing-on. At each interview the length of service required diminished. First it was 7 and 5 (seven years with the colours, five with the reserve), then 3 years, then 1 year, then finally a gentleman's agreement to stay on with the understanding that I could leave at any time if I felt I had had enough. The incentive was an immediate promotion to sergeant with further advancements to follow. I must confess to being tempted. I had enjoyed my service with the regiment, but I was keen to get home, where I had a guaranteed job, and I did not like the way the regimental life was going. The easy-going approach of the active service days had almost disappeared and I was never attracted to a life of parades, guard duties and general bull.

So I elected to go, and as my release group (47) was called, we were informed that we would be leaving for the UK at the end of the first week in January 1947. Reg Robinson, an old friend would be in the party.

The winter of 1946-47 was one of the most severe in recorded history and Austria had its fair share of its horrors. We had suffered icy roads, vehicles fitted with chains, draining-off radiators every evening and freezing barrack rooms. One morning I awoke to discover that my toothbrush was frozen solid in a mug of water at my bedside.

I had begun to prepare for demob and had commissioned a pair of civilian shoes from a local shoemaker. On the Saturday night after New Year I went to the Corporals' Mess for a drink. It was quiet, and after a couple of beers I decided to have an early night, and set off back. On the way, my new shoes with their shiny leather soles slipped on the icy road surface and I fell, banging my right ankle on the ground. The pain was so bad that I could hardly stand. Fortunately, a couple of passing soldiers helped me back to my hut, where I spent a sleepless and pain-filled night in an icy bed. On Sunday I went to the MI Room where a corporal bandaged my ankle and told me to report sick the next morning. Accordingly, I travelled into Klagenfurt where I saw an irascible Irish MO who pronounced, in his wisdom, that I had suffered some bad bruising but who decided it was best if he sent me to Klagenfurt General Hospital for a precautionary X-ray.

This involved a walk of a mile along icy pavements, then about a quarter of a mile of even icier driveway to the reception hall. After an X-ray, I was approached by the Austrian radiographer who informed me that I had a fracture. Almost immediately I was seized by two stalwarts of the Royal Army Medical Corps, lowered on to a stretcher and taken to a ward. There, a bed was prepared and I was placed tenderly therein, to await examination. Typical of the army—until my fracture had been diagnosed I was free, in fact, commanded to walk about for almost two days. Now I was forbidden to put foot to floor. The following morning my lower right leg was placed in plaster, with a sort of metal stirrup under the sole to enable me to walk. This meant that my right leg was some three inches longer than my left, which was remedied by screwing three inch blocks of wood to my left boot. It was like walking on stilts.

The following day I was visited by Reg and several other friends who were leaving the following day for the UK. I cannot adequately describe how I felt. I had been looking forward so much to this. A leave, then a return to Catterick to await 'demob', a cushy billet, a nice instructor's job for a few weeks, then home for good. Now I was consigned to a hospital bed among strangers and a seemingly endless wait for a return to health and 'demob'.

Within two days I was sent to a Convalescent Depot—the Schloss Hotel at Velden on the Worthersee. I had spent a leave in Velden in happier days, in the summer of 1946, and a very pleasant place it was.

Altogether I spent fourteen weeks there. It was a fine hotel and there was plenty of leisure facilities, a library, table tennis room, evening entertainments and superb food. I also met John Hart, convalescing from an appendectomy. His wife had gone off with another man and he was in the process of divorcing her. Whilst at the Convalescent Depot, he met an army nurse, also convalescing, and although he soon left on demob, they kept in touch and two years later were married. A welcome visitor at the hotel was my old friend, Lieutenant, now Captain Thorburn, who came to say goodbye before the regiment moved to Schleswig-Holstein.

As my ankle healed and the snow gave way to spring flowers I was able to indulge my passion for high-level walking and spent many happy afternoons exploring the tracks in the foothills above Velden.

In early May I was discharged and made my way across Europe and back to Britain with very little kit and hardly any personal possessions. The Red Cross gave me a drinking mug and eating utensils and I eventually arrived at Aldershot, where I spent one night before being taken to Woking to be kitted out with civilian clothes and to be officially 'demobbed'. After that I took a train to London followed by another one heading to the north-west of the country to Stockport. Now on very familiar ground I jumped on a bus to Gee Cross, Hyde and arrived home at last. It had been almost five years since I had left on my military adventures and now I was back at the point where it all started. I was a little weary and looked forward to doing absolutely nothing for a few weeks. So that is exactly what I did.

The British Army relinquished its principal claim upon me in August 1947 and relegated me to the ranks of the Territorial Army, 'Z' Reserve.

The world had changed. I had changed, but now it was time for another change.

There would be no more 'soldiering on' for me.

CHAPTER 17

Postscript: On Reflection

What effect, then, did the war have upon me?

I entered the army as little more than a schoolboy and left it as a mature man. I confirmed, to my own satisfaction, the truth of the cliché that we are all brothers under the skin. We all feel fear, relief, joy and a need for comradeship under stress.

I was fortunate in my parents, that they had no prejudices as far as nationality, race or colour were concerned and apart from teaching me the code of civilised conduct had not indoctrinated me with any opinions which they may have collected along the paths of their lives. Consequently, I had an open mind and my experiences have left me to this day without preconceptions of people—all I look for is how they behave towards me and society in general.

I was fortunate in being sent to the 16th/5th Lancers and 'B' Squadron in particular. I could not have wished to spend the war in the company of better men. With very few exceptions they were decent, honest and reliable companions, and the mutual affection and respect we held for each other is reflected in the fact that uniquely in the regiment, 'B' Squadron has had its own reunions since the 1950s. The original numbers of sixty or seventy have now shrunk to, at the last count, seven. Old age, infirmity and death have taken their toll, but our memories still remain.

A common complaint, and a justifiable one, I am sure, is that those of us who were around during the war keep banging on about it to the general boredom of those who were not then born. But it is worth bearing in mind that for everyone who lived through it, whether in the Forces or at home, in the factories and shops and homes, it was the biggest event and upheaval any of us is ever likely to endure. I feel that during the war the British people reached the height of their national qualities of moral fibre and dogged endurance. They were probably never as good before and in my opinion have certainly never been as good since those days.

There were many times during the Italian campaign that I felt proud to be British, and this a genuine claim and not merely a statement of jingoistic sentiment. There were many instances where the considerable extent of the respect in which we were held was made plain to us, largely due to the honourable conduct of our troops. The average British soldier showed himself to be a decent and compassionate man, even under conditions of extreme danger and it was a privilege to serve alongside him.

On the personal debit side, the war lost me five years of my youth, and found my position in civilian life frozen for the duration of hostilities. I left ICI as a junior cashier's clerk and resumed my employment as the most junior employee in the wages office. Although within four years I had been promoted to chief wages clerk, my options were very restricted, and I was 31 years of age before I passed my professional finals and became a qualified accountant—far too late for anyone with ambitions to become chairman of ICI.

Nevertheless, there was no point in grumbling about what might have been. It was not our way. Our expectations were not high, and material conditions had changed very little since the beginning of the century, only the invention of wireless and the development of the motorcar and the aeroplane having made any major change to our way of life. People were expected to get on with things without making a fuss and tended to keep their innermost emotions to themselves.

We had been exposed to dangers, had seen much of death and injury, and witnessed some appalling incidents, but we were given a 'demob' suit of clothes and a character reference and released into 'civvy street' as abruptly as we had been inducted into the army.

We were offered no counselling for coping with the abiding mental traumas of our experiences irrespective of their magnitude (it had not been dreamed of for soldiers at that time) and most of us would not have had it otherwise.

I certainly found no difficulty in settling back in to a civilian routine, although for the next couple of years I tended to jump at sudden loud bangs, and on walks in the country found myself weighing up the terrain to find suitable dips and hollows in which to take cover should the need, irrespective of the unlikelihood of such a possibility, again arise. Old habits die hard especially when they been learned for self-preservation.

It is a well-known fact that the mind tends to recall mainly pleasant memories from any situation and I feel that there is a danger when talking or writing about the war of giving the impression that it was all a barrel of fun. Rather, these amusing interludes were the much needed occasional bursts of light relief which illuminated the greater darkness. I hope that these memoirs will go some way to accurately portray the reality of what life was like for an ordinary soldier in a British tank regiment during the Second World War in a way which will benefit those who were not there and especially readers in future generations.

This book, of course, contains a very personal view of a tank soldiers war. To give the modern reader a useful overview of how the 16th/5th Lancers campaigned in Italy during the Second World War, this narrative has been appended with a detailed outline of the organisation of the regiment written by by one of our 'B' Squadron troop leaders, Henry Brooke, later both commanding officer and Colonel of the regiment. This organisation was originally published in the regimental journal, *The Scarlet and Green*, in 1985.

★★★★★★

I close with a reminder to everyone who has read this book and arrived at its conclusion with me now of the enormous contribution made by the many unhonoured and unsung ordinary citizen soldiers of the armoured regiments of the British Army during the Second World War 1939-45. This truth is accurately personified in the words of the regimental march of the Royal Tank Regiment:—

> *It wasn't the tanks that won the war*
> *It was my boy Willie*

CORPORAL SAM KNOWLES, 16TH/5TH LANCERS,
AUSTRIA 1945-6

The Organisation of the 16th/5th Lancers in the Italian Campaign in 1944 and 1945

Written in the 1985 *Regimental Journal* by
Colonel Henry Brooke MC, Troop
Leader in B Squadron 16/5L at the time

The aim of this article is to give the reader some idea of how the 16th/5th Lancers (16/5L) were organised and administered during the Italian Campaign of 1944 and 1945. When the Regimental History was written in 1961, 16/5L was still an armoured regiment and squadron leaders had served in the war. It was not therefore necessary to describe how the Regiment functioned during the latter part of the war. Now, twelve years after becoming a reconnaissance regiment, it is only the squadron leaders who have any experience of an armoured regiment's organisation; it therefore seems an opportune time to record the details of the armoured regiment in war as it was in 1944 and 1945.

THE OFFICIAL ESTABLISHMENT

The Regiment was on an establishment known as WE 11/151/3 and consisted of 37 Officers and 627 other ranks from the Royal Armoured Corps (RAC), 19 from the Army Catering Corps (ACC), and 9 from the Royal Electrical and Mechanical Engineers (REME). The Light Aid Detachment REME (LAD) was a separate establishment and included one

190

officer and 25 other ranks attached to the Regiment. The Strength Return for May 1944 (the Battle for Cassino) was 35 officers, 649 other ranks 16/5L, 19 ACC, four REME, and the LAD was one officer and 22 other ranks.

At the start of the Italian campaign the Regiment was under-implemented as the Light Anti-Aircraft tanks were never issued but the strength did include first line reinforcements. It has not been possible to find an accurate strength return for a fighting squadron (known as a sabre squadron) but it would have consisted of eight officers and about 160 other ranks. This is much larger, of course, than today's squadrons primarily because the Sherman tank had a five-man crew and so 90 men were required to man the tanks. Another 20-30 men were the spare crews who travelled with the echelon but were fully tank trained and filled in the gaps when crews suffered battle casualties. In the echelon they acted as co-drivers of the support vehicles (B vehicles) and also helped to manhandle the ammunition (ammo) and petrol, oil and lubricants (POL).

ADMINISTRATIVE ORGANISATION

The Regiment had 61 Sherman and 11 Honey tanks and was divided into the following for administrative purposes:

Headquarter Squadron (HQ Sqn)

Regimental Headquarters Troop (RHQ Tp)
- 4 Sherman tanks

Reconnaissance Troop (Recce Tp)
- 11 Honey tanks

Intercommunication Troop (Intercom Tp)
- 10 scout cars

Despatch Rider Troop (DR Tp)

Technical Adjutant's Troop (Tech Adjt Tp)

Quartermaster's Troop (QM Tp)

Motor Transport Troop (MT Tp)

Fitters Troop (Fitters)

Administrative Troop (Admin Tp)

Medical Troop - Regimental Aid Post (RAP)

Three Sabre Squadrons (A, B and C Sqns)

Each consisting of 19 Shermans and divided into:
Squadron Headquarters Troop (SHQ Tp) - 4 Shermans
1st Troop (1 Tp)
2nd Troop (2 Tp)
3rd Troop (3 Tp)
4th Troop (4 Tp)
Fitters Troop (Fitters)
Motor Transport Troop (MT Tp)
Administrative Troop (Admin Tp)

The official establishment was for five troops of three Shermans each, but the regiment adopted its own organisation where each squadron had four troops, three of four Shermans and one of three.

Light Aid Detachment REME (LAD)

The LAD was attached to 16/5L but on a separate establishment and the members of the various Fitter Troops were 16th/5th Lancers.

OPERATIONAL ORGANISATION

Operationally the Regiment was organised as follows:
Fighting Echelon   (F Ech)
A1 Echelon   (A1 Ech)
A2 Echelon   (A2 Ech)
B Echelon   (B Ech)

Each Squadron had about 15 B vehicles which included a jeep, two 15 hundredweight (cwt) trucks, 10 three-ton trucks and stores binned trucks. The fitters troop, who were all 16th/5th Lancers, numbered 12 and together with the regimental cooks, squadron clerks, pay clerk, medical orderly, squadron quarter master sergeant (SQMS) and his men, would bring the squadron total to about 160 men. This left nearly 200 all ranks in regimental headquarters (RHQ) and HQ Squadron.

HONEY TANK AND 12 RHA OP TANK

12 RHA 105MM PRIEST

THE FIGHTING ECHELON

The fighting part of the Regiment varied in detail depending on what sort of action the Regiment was expecting, but the following would be a typical order of battle (ORBAT):

RHQ

Vehicles	Officers
4 Shermans	Commanding Officer
2 Honeys	Second in Command
Scout Cars	Adjutant
Jeeps	Intelligence Officer
	Reconnaissance Troop Leader
1 Sherman	Battery Commander, 12 RHA
1 Scout Car	Troop Commander,
	Field Engineer Squadron

Sabre Squadrons, each:

Squadron Headquarters	
4 Shermans	Squadron Leader
	Second in Command
1 Scout Car	Rear Link Captain
1 Sherman (12 RHA)	Forward Observation Officer
(or called OP Tank)	(FOO)
1,2 and 3 Tps, each	
4 Shermans	Tank Commanders:
	Troop Leader
	Troop Sergeant
	Sergeant
	Corporal
4 Tp	
3 Shermans	Troop Leader
	Sergeant
	Corporal
Section Recce Tp	
3 Honeys	
Fitter Tp	
Armoured Recovery	Moving on Sqn Ldr's orders

Vehicle (ARV)	and possibly based in Al Ech
White Half Track	
Ambulance	As for above vehicles
White Scout Car	

A1 ECHELON

This was the regiment's emergency reserve and moved under RHQ's orders. Second in Command (2i/c) HQ Squadron normally commanded A1. It had one POL lorry and one ammo lorry from each squadron.

A2 ECHELON

This was the main echelon and was responsible for supplying F Echelon each day with all their fuel and ammunition requirements. It was commanded by headquarter squadron leader and each squadron detachment was commanded by the Squadron Sergeant Major (SSM) or SQMS. The echelon was moved under control of divisional headquarters. The actual POL and ammo to be brought forward, and the map reference, were given out by RHQ every afternoon. Each squadron echelon might consist of over ten B vehicles, mostly three-tonners. Often there was a spare tank waiting to join the squadron, on the squadron leader's instructions. The quartermaster was based on A2.

INDEPENDENTS

There were a number of people who might be in one of several places depending on the situation. An example was the technical adjutant who might be in A2, A1 or even RHQ, depending on what recovery of tanks was required.

B ECHELON

In theory the whole regiment was mobile, but in practice this was not the case. Such things as tentage, .50 Browning machine guns (from the cupolas of the Shermans) and much other equipment not required for battle, were dumped in a suitable site with a small party and a few vehicles. It was necessary to unload A1 Echelon to move B Echelon, and so it was moved only as often as necessary.

'B' SQUADRON, 75MM SHERMAN TANK, APRIL 1945

12 RHA OP TANK ON LEFT AND 75MM SHERMAN, MAY 1945

SHERMAN ARV

THE VEHICLES

The Sherman Tank

The Regiment started the campaign with diesel Shermans with 75mm guns, very similar to the illustrations. Extra armour plates were welded to the sides of the tanks outside the ammunition bins, and racks were welded on the back of the engine plate (there were no engine doors on our Shermans) to take bedding, water and cooking fuel. In the summer of 1944 two Shermans in each squadron headquarters were replaced by Shermans with 105mm guns. In 1945, before the final battle, troops were reduced to three tanks, each with two of the improved version of the Sherman mounting a 75mm gun and the third an old type mounting a 17pdr British gun.

The Honey Tank

The reconaissance troop had Honeys which were American Light Tanks mounting a 37mm gun. All the Honeys in the armoured brigade had their turrets taken off and a machine gun was mounted on the turret ring. The troop, known as Honey Troop, was trained in mine laying and clearance, demolitions and their clearance, and route reconnaissance. It was also used to evacuate casualties and bring up POL and Ammo whenever the echelon could not get up to the tanks. A section of three Honeys was normally allocated to each squadron and two Honeys travelled with RHQ.

The Scout Car

The Regiment had a mixture of Daimler scout cars (the crew of two sat side-by-side) and Humber scout cars. They were used by liaison officers and generally for those needing to move on roads liable to be shelled.

Recovery and Fitters Vehicles

Each squadron had an armoured recovery vehicle (ARV) based on the Sherman chassis with a jib. This was used to recover damaged and bogged tanks. A White Half Track carried the vehicle mechanics who repaired all the squadron vehicles. In addition, each squadron had a binned lorry for tank spare parts and a battery charging vehicle.

Echelon Vehicles

The majority of the Regiment's logistic vehicles were three-ton trucks with two-wheel drive, either Bedford or Ford. Most of the 15cwts trucks had four-wheel drive, as of course did all the Jeeps. All the three-ton ammunition and POL vehicles had their canopies taken off and left in B Echelon during operations.

ORGANISATION OF 6TH (BRITISH) ARMOURED DIVISION IN ITALY, 1944

Having gone into the regimental organisation in some detail it may be useful to look at the part the Regiment played in 6th Armoured Division, whose organisation is shown below:

26th Armoured Brigade
> 16th/5th Lancers
> 17th/21st Lancers
> 2nd Lothians and Border Horse
> (10th Battalion The Rifle Brigade) (to Jun 44)

1st Guards Brigade
> 3rd Battalion Grenadier Guards
> 2nd Battalion Coldstream Guards
> 3rd Battalion Welsh Guards

61st Lorried Infantry Brigade (from Jun 44)
> (1st Battalion King's Royal Rifle Corps)
>> (from Feb 45)
> 2nd Battalion The Rifle Brigade
> 7th Battalion The Rifle Brigade
> (10th Battalion The Rifle Brigade)
>> (Jun 44 to Feb 45, then disbanded)

Artillery
> 12th Regiment Royal Horse Artillery
> 2nd Honourable Artillery Company (12 RHA)
>> 24 – SP 105mm guns (Priests)
> Field Regiment
>> 24 – Towed 25pdr guns (with 61 Bde)

16TH/5TH LANCERS 75MM SHERMAN TANK ENTERING AREZZO,
16 JULY 1944

The Ayrshire Yeomanry
24 - Towed 25pdr guns
72nd Anti-Tank Regiment
36 - SP 76mm guns (M10)
40th Light Anti-Aircraft Regiment
54 – Towed 40mm Bofors

Engineers

Field Engineer Squadron
Field Engineer Squadron
(Field Engineer Squadron)
Field Park Squadron

Reconnaissance

2nd Derbyshire Yeomanry

H.A.G.B

LEONAUR

ALSO FROM LEONAUR
AVAILABLE IN SOFTCOVER OR HARDCOVER WITH DUST JACKET

THE 9TH—THE KING'S (LIVERPOOL REGIMENT) IN THE GREAT WAR 1914 - 1918 *by Enos H. G. Roberts*—Mersey to mud—war and Liverpool men.

THE GAMBARDIER *by Mark Severn*—The experiences of a battery of Heavy artillery on the Western Front during the First World War.

FROM MESSINES TO THIRD YPRES *by Thomas Floyd*—A personal account of the First World War on the Western front by a 2/5th Lancashire Fusilier.

THE IRISH GUARDS IN THE GREAT WAR - VOLUME 1 *by Rudyard Kipling*—Edited and Compiled from Their Diaries and Papers—The First Battalion.

THE IRISH GUARDS IN THE GREAT WAR - VOLUME 1 *by Rudyard Kipling*—Edited and Compiled from Their Diaries and Papers—The Second Battalion.

ARMOURED CARS IN EDEN *by K. Roosevelt*—An American President's son serving in Rolls Royce armoured cars with the British in Mesopatamia & with the American Artillery in France during the First World War.

CHASSEUR OF 1914 *by Marcel Dupont*—Experiences of the twilight of the French Light Cavalry by a young officer during the early battles of the great war in Europe.

TROOP HORSE & TRENCH *by R.A. Lloyd*—The experiences of a British Lifeguardsman of the household cavalry fighting on the western front during the First World War 1914-18.

THE EAST AFRICAN MOUNTED RIFLES *by C.J. Wilson*—Experiences of the campaign in the East African bush during the First World War.

THE LONG PATROL *by George Berrie*—A Novel of Light Horsemen from Gallipoli to the Palestine campaign of the First World War.

THE FIGHTING CAMELIERS *by Frank Reid*—The exploits of the Imperial Camel Corps in the desert and Palestine campaigns of the First World War.

STEEL CHARIOTS IN THE DESERT *by S. C. Rolls*—The first world war experiences of a Rolls Royce armoured car driver with the Duke of Westminster in Libya and in Arabia with T.E. Lawrence.

WITH THE IMPERIAL CAMEL CORPS IN THE GREAT WAR *by Geoffrey Inchbald*—The story of a serving officer with the British 2nd battalion against the Senussi and during the Palestine campaign.

LEONAUR

ALSO FROM LEONAUR
AVAILABLE IN SOFTCOVER OR HARDCOVER WITH DUST JACKET

ESCAPE FROM THE FRENCH by Edward Boys—A Young Royal Navy Midshipman's Adventures During the Napoleonic War.

THE VOYAGE OF H.M.S. PANDORA by Edward Edwards R. N. & George Hamilton, edited by Basil Thomson—In Pursuit of the Mutineers of the Bounty in the South Seas—1790-1791.

MEDUSA by J. B. Henry Savigny and Alexander Correard and Charlotte-Adélaïde Dard —Narrative of a Voyage to Senegal in 1816 & The Sufferings of the Picard Family After the Shipwreck of the Medusa.

THE SEA WAR OF 1812 VOLUME 1 by A. T. Mahan—A History of the Maritime Conflict.

THE SEA WAR OF 1812 VOLUME 2 by A. T. Mahan—A History of the Maritime Conflict.

WETHERELL OF H. M. S. HUSSAR by John Wetherell—The Recollections of an Ordinary Seaman of the Royal Navy During the Napoleonic Wars.

THE NAVAL BRIGADE IN NATAL by C. R. N. Burne—With the Guns of H. M. S. Terrible & H. M. S. Tartar during the Boer War 1899-1900.

THE VOYAGE OF H. M. S. BOUNTY by William Bligh—The True Story of an 18th Century Voyage of Exploration and Mutiny.

SHIPWRECK! by William Gilly—The Royal Navy's Disasters at Sea 1793-1849.

KING'S CUTTERS AND SMUGGLERS: 1700-1855 by E. Keble Chatterton—A unique period of maritime history-from the beginning of the eighteenth to the middle of the nineteenth century when British seamen risked all to smuggle valuable goods from wool to tea and spirits from and to the Continent.

CONFEDERATE BLOCKADE RUNNER by John Wilkinson—The Personal Recollections of an Officer of the Confederate Navy.

NAVAL BATTLES OF THE NAPOLEONIC WARS by W. H. Fitchett—Cape St.Vincent, the Nile, Cadiz, Copenhagen, Trafalgar & Others.

PRISONERS OF THE RED DESERT by R. S. Gwatkin-Williams—The Adventures of the Crew of the Tara During the First World War.

U-BOAT WAR 1914-1918 by James B. Connolly/Karl von Schenk—Two Contrasting Accounts from Both Sides of the Conflict at Sea During the Great War.

Lightning Source UK Ltd.
Milton Keynes UK
UKHW021811020219
336574UK00001B/59/P

9 781782 826057